Cambrid

Richard S

Elektra

The contributors to this handbook bring together the first full-length study of *Elektra* in English. The volume examines the many facets of one of Richard Strauss's most complex operas. First, P. E. Easterling surveys the mythological background, while Karen Forsyth discusses Hofmannsthal's adaptation of his sources. The second part of the book brings the music to the fore. Derrick Puffett offers an introductory essay and synopsis; Arnold Whittall considers the tonal and dramatic structure of the composition; and Tethys Carpenter explores the musical language of the work in detail, with special focus given to part of the Klytämnestra scene. The third part of the volume offers two contrasting critical essays: Carolyn Abbate provides an interpretation of music and language in the work, and Robin Holloway analyses Strauss's orchestration.

The book also contains a discography, bibliography and illustrations.

CAMBRIDGE OPERA HANDBOOKS

Published titles

Richard Strauss
Elektra

Edited by
DERRICK PUFFETT

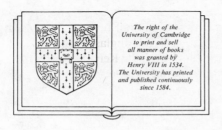

The right of the
University of Cambridge
to print and sell
all manner of books
was granted by
Henry VIII in 1534.
The University has printed
and published continuously
since 1584.

CAMBRIDGE UNIVERSITY PRESS

Cambridge
New York   Port Chester
Melbourne   Sydney

Published by the Press Syndicate of the University of Cambridge
The Pitt Building, Trumpington Street, Cambridge CB2 1RP
40 West 20th Street, New York, NY 10011, USA
10 Stamford Road, Oakleigh, Melbourne 3166, Australia

First published 1989

Printed in Great Britain at the University Press, Cambridge

British Library cataloguing in publication data

Richard Strauss: 'Elektra'. – (Cambridge opera
handbooks)
1. Opera in German. Strauss, Richard, 1864–
1949. Elektra
I. Puffett, Derrick
782.1′092′4

Library of Congress cataloguing in publication data

Richard Strauss, Elektra / edited by Derrick Puffett.
    p.   cm. – (Cambridge opera handbooks)
Bibliography.
Discography.
Includes index.
ISBN 0–521–35173–1. – ISBN 0–521–35971–6 (pbk.)
1. Strauss, Richard, 1864–1949.   Elektra.   I. Puffett, Derrick.
II. Title: Elektra.   III. Series.
ML410.S93R485 1989
782.1′092′4 – dc19   89–499 CIP

ISBN 0 521 35173 1 hard covers
ISBN 0 521 35971 6 paperback

ME

Contents

Illustrations

General preface

This is a series of studies of individual operas written for the opera-goer or record-collector as well as the student or scholar. Each volume has three main concerns: historical, analytical and interpretative. There is a detailed description of the genesis of each work, and of the collaboration between librettist and composer. A full synopsis considers the opera as a structure of musical and dramatic effects, and there is also a musical analysis of a section of the score. The analysis, like the history, shades naturally into interpretation: by a careful combination of new essays and excerpts from classic statements the editors of the handbooks show how critical writing about the opera, like the production and performance, can direct or distort appreciation of its structural elements. A final section of documents gives a select bibliography, a discography, and guides to other sources. Each book is published both in hard covers and as a paperback.

For K.

Introduction

I

This book is intended as a companion to the *Salome* volume in the same series. They were written concurrently, call on some of the same contributors and share the same concerns – notably an emphasis on the music (as opposed to questions of historical background, performance tradition and so on, though all of these are covered to some extent). The emphasis on the music was a matter of deliberate choice. There are plenty of books on Strauss's operas – those by William Mann and Norman Del Mar will be most familiar to the English-speaking reader[1] – as well as studies of individual works.[2] Strauss's music, however, has never enjoyed the sustained analytical attention given to works by other composers of his generation, such as Mahler and Schoenberg. As a result, critical comment tends to remain rather general. There is simply no need for another 'introduction' to works such as *Salome* and *Elektra* (which in any case are part of the standard operatic repertory, not to mention the many fine recordings). What is needed is to raise the level of critical debate. The two handbooks are intended as a modest step in this direction.

Elektra has never of course been *neglected* critically, as *Salome* has. Its reputation is summed up in Stravinsky's remark: 'Since *Parsifal* there have been only two operas, *Elektra* and *Pelléas*.'[3] Though certainly not the last work – not even the last work of Strauss's – to enter the standard repertory, it is the only one of his to enjoy almost unqualified critical success in recent times, a startling change of fortune when the earliest reviews are taken into account. Stravinsky's praise is the more impressive coming from someone who detested Strauss and all he stood for. Anton Webern, a pupil of Schoenberg and therefore 'on the other side of the fence' so far as modern music was concerned, had to admit that 'there does exist in Strauss such an immense virtuosity in everything, which Pfitzner and

1

Reger, for instance, do not possess'[4] (admittedly he was not talking specifically about *Elektra* here). And Kurt Weill, who dismissed a number of Strauss operas as being derived from Wagner, nevertheless admired the musical innovations of *Elektra*.[5]

But many of those who disapprove of *Salome* and/or Strauss in general make an exception of *Elektra*, a curious state of affairs given that *Salome* is arguably the more successful work. Perhaps it is simply because *Elektra* is based on a Greek tragedy, a far more respectable pedigree than the dubious Wilde. A more likely reason is found in the shifting value systems that characterise twentieth-century art. *Elektra*, at first criticised for its modernity, is now admired because it is 'progressive': this was certainly part of Adorno's thinking when he described the Klytämnestra scene as 'the climax of Strauss's work' (in the context of a bitter attack on the composer's music as a whole).[6] Max Deutsch, another Schoenberg pupil, gave a memorable series of classes on *Elektra* in Paris in the 1950s.[7] And Carl Dahlhaus, the *éminence grise* of modern German musicology and no admirer of Strauss, devotes three pages to the work in his history of nineteenth-century music.[8] If not exactly well liked, *Elektra* seems to have become a classic.

The work has also attracted the attention of distinguished Germanists, being, of course, the first in the remarkable series of collaborations between Strauss and the Austrian poet and playwright Hugo von Hofmannsthal. Writing on *Elektra*, then, is hardly meagre. And it is probably fair to say that, even in the relatively undistinguished field of Strauss studies, *Elektra* tends to bring out the best in its commentators. Among British authors, both Mann and Del Mar devote their finest chapters to the work: whatever their expressed reservations (Del Mar in particular seems to find it distasteful),[9] they write with vigour and perceptiveness. There is also a major study by the Austrian musicologist Kurt Overhoff.[10]

All this is a far cry from the reviews that greeted the first performances. *Salome* had caused a scandal in 1905.[11] Now Strauss was abused again (no doubt to his delight) as decadent and immoral, the 'Barnum of German music'. Thomas San-Galli, author of a biography of Brahms, wrote in the *Rheinische Musik- und Theaterzeitung* that *Elektra* was a work 'that one has to have heard, however unpleasant the experience may be. Then it will sink into oblivion quickly and for ever.'[12] Others could not believe that the work was meant seriously.[13] Cartoons appeared in the newspapers depicting Strauss as a musical sadist, with Hofmannsthal his accomplice.[14] There were satirical references to libretti for 'opera composers of Straussian tendencies', with titles such as 'Incest', 'Lynch Justice' and 'The Bloodthirsty Gorilla'.[15] Naturally the Klytämnestra scene came in for special criticism, on account of its supposed 'atonality': 'It is complete anarchy', wrote Willy Pastor in the *Tägliche Rundschau*.[16]

A few critics were more perceptive. Writing in the *Münchner neuesten Nachrichten*, Alexander Dillmann praised the work as 'purer and more authentic than much of what is written according to the rule-book. . . . Of this there can be no doubt: *Elektra* represents a decisive milestone in music history.' At the end of his review Dillmann responded to criticisms of the Klytämnestra scene:

Let the esteemed reader sit at the piano and [play] . . . two *Elektra*-chords: E flat in the bass, C–D–F sharp–A in the middle register left hand, E sharp–B–C sharp–G in the right hand. This 'resolves' to E flat–G–C–E–G–B flat in the left hand, F sharp–A sharp–C sharp–F sharp in the right! That is a small sample from the Klytämnestra scene [the four bars before Fig. 193: see also Chapter 6, Ex. 8]. On the piano it does indeed sound a little surprising. But in the orchestra the colours are mixed to such an extent that the dissonance is hardly perceptible as such, merely as an illustration of Klytämnestra's words. Also we get a quite different sense of the organic connection between these chords in the orchestra than we do from the vocal score, which is in many respects nothing short of a caricature of the real tonal image.[17]

And the first performances in London (1910, as part of the first Beecham season at Covent Garden) seem to have been an almost total success.[18]

II

The story of the events leading up to the première has been told many times, but it still retains its interest. After the première of *Salome*, on 9 December 1905, Strauss was at something of a loss. He was at the height of his career both as a composer and as a conductor (since 1898 he had held the much-coveted position of Kapellmeister of the Berlin Court Opera). He would have liked to write a comic opera, but no suitable subject suggested itself; and he was bored with writing symphonic poems.[19] With a certain sense of resignation – and a few misgivings about embarking upon a subject so outwardly similar to that of his last success – he asked Hofmannsthal for permission to adapt his *Elektra*.[20]

The two artists had met in 1899, at the home of Richard Dehmel in Berlin-Pankow.[21] In March the following year they met again in Paris, to discuss the scenario for a possible ballet, *Der Triumph der*

Zeit. Hofmannsthal wrote it,[22] but Strauss was already involved with a ballet of his own (the never-completed *Kythere*) and did not want to commit himself to another so soon.[23] He was also busy on the opera *Feuersnot*. Then came *Salome*, which occupied him from 1902 – when he saw Max Reinhardt's production, with Gertrud Eysoldt, at Reinhardt's Kleines Theater in Berlin – to 1905. In 1903 or 1904[24] he saw Hofmannsthal's newly-completed *Elektra*, again with Eysoldt, at the Kleines Theater. It was *Salome* all over again: as he wrote in his 'Reminiscences of the First Performance of My Operas' (1942), 'I immediately recognised . . . what a magnificent operatic libretto it might be'.[25]

After the *Salome* première he communicated his enthusiasm about *Elektra* to its author (whether by letter or in person we do not know).[26] The first letter that pertains to *Elektra* in the surviving correspondence is dated 7 March 1906.[27] A certain amount of wooing was necessary before Strauss would finally commit himself: in particular he had to be reassured that the similarities to *Salome* were only superficial. Hofmannsthal, clearly excited about the prospect of working with Germany's leading composer, tried to put his mind at rest:

(Both are one-act plays; each has a woman's name for a title; both take place in classical antiquity, and both parts were originally created in Berlin by Gertrud Eysoldt; that, I feel, is all the similarity adds up to.) The blend of colour in the two subjects strikes me as quite different in all essentials; in *Salome* much is so to speak purple and violet, the atmosphere is torrid; in *Elektra*, on the other hand, it is a mixture of night and light, or black and bright. What is more, the rapid rising sequence of events relating to Orestes and his deed which leads up to victory and purification – a sequence which I can imagine much more powerful in music than in the written word – is not matched by anything of a corresponding, or even faintly similar kind in *Salome*.[28]

The suggestion that music could capture 'the rapid rising sequence of events' much more powerfully than the written word was high praise indeed for Hofmannsthal.[29] Nevertheless it was only when the financial details were agreed that Strauss began work on the composition.

On 16 June 1906 he wrote to Hofmannsthal that he was 'already busy on the first scene'.[30] From then on things went fairly smoothly. (The details of the collaboration are discussed by Karen Forsyth below.)[31] There was a small hiccup in September, when the news that Strauss was working on *Elektra* – until then a closely guarded secret – leaked into the press (this was naturally a matter of worldwide interest). Hofmannsthal hastened to assure the composer that he was not to blame. Strauss's next surviving letter is dated 22 December 1907 and makes no reference to the matter.

The actual composition of the work proceeded slowly, owing to Strauss's extensive conducting commitments. There were also compositional difficulties: it seems that either Elektra's monologue or the Klytämnestra scene was rewritten twice.[32] Nevertheless Strauss played the Klytämnestra scene to Mahler at one of their last meetings, possibly as early as December 1906.[33] This would appear to have been a painful occasion for Mahler, largely because Strauss omitted to ask him about his own music. He wrote to Alma:

Strauss has already composed a number of scenes from *Elektra* (Hofmannsthal). He won't part with it for less than 10 per cent per evening and 100,000 marks. (That is just my guess, I admit.) As he did not inquire, I did not tell him anything about my antiquated existence this summer [setting the Latin hymn *Veni creator spiritus* as part of his Eighth Symphony]. I doubt whether he would be much impressed to hear with what quaint relics I occupy my summer. Oh, how blissful to be modern.[34]

His reaction to *Elektra* was straightforwardly negative.[35] Strauss received a much more cheering response from Hofmannsthal when he played him extracts in December 1906 and February 1908.[36]

The distractions were severe. In the winter of 1907–8 Strauss had to be in Paris (for six performances of *Salome*, which he himself conducted), Vienna (for concerts with the Vienna Philharmonic) and Rome. In May 1908 he took the Berlin Philharmonic Orchestra on tour to France, Spain, Portugal, Italy, Switzerland and southern Germany, conducting thirty-one concerts in as many days. In August he spent a week at a Strauss Festival in Wiesbaden.[37] Relief came at last in October, when he was promoted to Generalmusikdirektor and granted a year's leave of absence. This was too late to help with the composition of *Elektra*, which bears the finishing-date '22 September 1908'. But it did mean that his next opera, *Der Rosenkavalier*, could proceed more swiftly.

Strauss seems to have decided at an early stage – perhaps as early as 1907 – that the première would be in Dresden. It had been Dresden, after all, that took a risk with *Salome* (as well as the earlier *Feuersnot*), and Hofmannsthal, too, wanted to avoid a possible failure in Vienna.[38] On 11 September (1908) he told the conductor, Ernst von Schuch, that the score was ready: 'The end is juicy! The principal role must now undoubtedly be given to the most highly dramatic soprano you have.' Then, on 6 January 1909: 'I am wildly eager to hear the *Elektra* orchestra for the first time on the 18th.'[39] The actual première was on 25 January. As usual, Strauss had planned things like a military operation: *Elektra* would be the first event in a four-day festival, with *Salome* following on the 26th, *Feuersnot* on the 27th (together with the *Symphonia Domestica*) and a second performance of *Elektra* on the 28th (see the poster reproduced as Plate 1). The singers were some of the best he ever had: Annie Krull (a performer he later singled out for special praise) in the title role, Margarethe Siems as Chrysothemis, Carl Perron as Orestes and Ernestine Schumann-Heinck (a veteran Wagnerian and the only one of his performers about whom Strauss had reservations) as Klytämnestra. The conductor was conscientious almost to a fault.[40]

Despite all these preparations, *Elektra* was no more than a *succès d'estime*, as Strauss wrote rather nonchalantly in his reminiscences, adding that 'as usual, I did not learn this until later'.[41] Angelo Neumann even telegraphed to Prague that it had 'flopped'. Perhaps the critics had been more effective than they had been with *Salome*. Perhaps the public simply recognised that the work was flawed. At all events the performances that followed in Munich, Frankfurt, Berlin, Vienna, Graz, Cologne, Hamburg and elsewhere saw a gradual revival in its fortunes. By 21 April 1909, after a successful performance in Milan, Strauss could write to his librettist: 'I think we've now definitely turned the corner with *Elektra*.'[42]

III

A book on *Elektra* is necessarily more heterogeneous than one on *Salome*. This is because of certain qualities in the work itself. Whereas in *Salome* Strauss seems to have been trying to achieve a kind of organicism,[43] he was attracted to *Elektra* by its contrasts: his claim that '*Elektra* became even more intense in the unity of structure'[44] shows his awareness of the possible problems. And *Elektra* does have problems, whatever its apologists may say: the discontinuity of style from one scene to another, the uneven quality of the musical ideas, the sheer bombast of the ending.[45] Moreover, there is a certain open-ended quality about it, an incompleteness, which has to do with the nature of the myth. As William Mann observes, 'the mythological Electra did not die',[46] just as Chrysothemis and Orestes lived on to see the rise of a new generation. Although nothing could seem more final than the hammering chords at the end

1: The poster for the première of *Elektra*: Königliches Opernhaus, Dresden, 25 January 1909

of Strauss's opera, there is something deeply disturbing about the image of Chrysothemis beating at the door. The last word in Hofmannsthal's libretto, before '*Curtain*', is '*Silence*' (*Stille*): the lack of response to Chrysothemis' beating means that the story is not yet over.

This 'open-ended quality' was bound to impose itself on the book whether I wanted it to or not. In fact I deliberately chose contributors who would reflect the different aspects of the work through their differing styles and approaches. (With such a many-sided work, in any case, it seemed important to find writers who were *specialists* in each of the different fields – a classicist, a Germanist and so on – rather than to try to achieve a collective view.) And though I hope that the essays complement one another, at least to the extent of providing the sort of comprehensive survey that is customary in the Cambridge Opera Handbooks series, I take pleasure in the fact that the *style* of Robin Holloway, for example, is as different as possible from that of Karen Forsyth (as is his attitude to Hofmannsthal), just as the analytical style of Arnold Whittall is very different from my own. Still less than in the case of *Salome* was there any possibility of coming to a 'conclusion'.

The general layout of the book, nevertheless, follows the usual pattern for the series. First P. E. Easterling surveys the mythological background, while Karen Forsyth discusses Hofmannsthal's adaptation of his sources (her emphasis on Sophocles is particularly original and interesting). The second part of the book brings the music to the fore. I offer some preliminary thoughts and a synopsis; then Arnold Whittall considers the tonal and dramatic structure; finally Tethys Carpenter explores the musical language of the work in greater detail (she also analyses part of the Klytämnestra scene). The third part of the book offers two contrasting critical essays: by Carolyn Abbate, whose interpretation is informed by her recent work on narrative, and by Robin Holloway, who seems to have founded a new genre – a critical study of a work through its orchestration. The only aspect of the work that I thought it necessary to omit was its stage history: until very recent times a realistic staging was evidently considered *de rigueur*,[47] and a description of so many similar productions would have been tedious and unilluminating. As usual in the series, the discography is by Malcolm Walker.

Certain linguistic inconsistencies have proved unavoidable. I have tried to distinguish between Electra and Elektra, and between Clytemnestra and Klytämnestra, where the former refers to the character in a general, mythological sense and the latter to the character in Strauss/Hofmannsthal. Aegisthus and Orestes, on the other hand, are used in preference to Aegisth and Orest (except where the context makes it impossible) because of their greater familiarity to the English-speaking reader. The other characters present no problem.

Note: The orchestral and vocal scores of *Elektra* are published by Boosey & Hawkes (1943) © copyright 1908 by Adolph Fürstner. Copyright assigned 1943 to Boosey & Hawkes Ltd., for all countries excluding Germany, Danzig, Italy, Portugal and the U.S.S.R. Reprinted by permission of Boosey & Hawkes Music Publishers Ltd. References to specific passages are given in the form 'four bars after Fig. 101', often abbreviated to 'Fig. 101/4'. In such references the bar headed by the rehearsal number is always included.

1   *Electra's story*

P. E. EASTERLING

> Sometime let gorgeous Tragedy
> In sceptred pall come sweeping by,
> Presenting Thebes, or Pelops' line,
> Or the tale of Troy divine.   Milton, *Il Penseroso*

As a descendant of Pelops, Electra belongs to one of the most
notable families of Greek heroic myth: her father was Agamemnon,
king of Argos and Mycenae, her mother Clytemnestra, her sister
Iphigenia and her brother Orestes. Between them they provided the
subject-matter for some of the most famous plays composed at
Athens during the great creative period of Greek tragedy, and
through tragedy they have inspired countless later writers from
Seneca to Sartre. Earlier generations of the family had also con-
tributed their share of remarkable or ghastly deeds: Tantalus, who
cut up his own son Pelops and served him at a divine feast, in order
to test the powers of the immortals; Pelops himself, who won a bride
by a treacherous act of cunning and was cursed, along with all his
progeny, by the accomplice he had later abandoned; his sons Atreus
and Thyestes, paradigms of sibling rivalry, whose quarrel lay behind
the story of Agamemnon's death. Aegisthus, son of Thyestes and
lover of Clytemnestra, had more than one reason for wishing Agamemnon dead: it was Agamemnon's father Atreus who had but-
chered some of Thyestes' less fortunate children and served them to
him at a banquet, in revenge for Thyestes' adultery with his wife;
but Aegisthus, the youngest, escaped and lived to see his father
avenged through new acts of adultery and murder.

These and large numbers of other stories had been told long
before the tragedies were composed in the fifth century B.C.: they
belonged to the extraordinarily rich repertoire of oral poetry, developed and handed down over many generations, which was at its most
flourishing and widespread during the eighth, seventh and sixth centuries. Of all the great range of long narrative poems that we know to

have existed, only the *Iliad* and the *Odyssey* have survived complete; there were many others, more or less totally lost to us, on different phases in the history of the Trojan War, on the expedition of Jason and the Argonauts, the labours of Heracles, and the doings of the Theban royal family, Laius, Oedipus and his fratricidal sons. Nor was this all: many of the vases that survive from the time of the tragedians or earlier are painted with scenes from stories about these people, but stories that do not always tally with the literary tradition as we have it. Evidently there was plenty of room for variation: the notion of a strictly 'canonical' version is alien to Greek ways of thinking, and we have to remember that these traditions of storytelling and oral poetry were spread over a wide geographical area with different local interests. Many of the stories were associated with particular cities, their cults and their leading families; we ought not to be surprised if the record turns out to be less tidy than a superficial glance at a handbook of Greek mythology might suggest.[1]

The story of Electra illustrates the point well. Her family is very prominent in Homer: Agamemnon, after all, was leader of the Greek expedition to Troy, and the dreadful story of his homecoming, when he was treacherously killed by Aegisthus (or Aegisthus and Clytemnestra) on his victorious return from his Trojan conquest, is told several times in the *Odyssey* as a contrast to the story of Odysseus and his faithful Penelope.[2] Orestes, too, receives attention as the son who comes back from exile to avenge his father's death.[3] Yet there is no word of Electra, no hint of a reunion between brother and sister or of their shared participation in the killing of Clytemnestra and Aegisthus. In the *Iliad*, indeed, where specific mention is made of Agamemnon's daughters, Electra's name does not appear in the list. In Book 9, when Agamemnon is hoping that Achilles will be persuaded to come back into the fighting, he offers a choice of one of his daughters as Achilles' bride:

> I have three daughters in my well-built palace,
> Chrysothemis and Laodice and Iphianassa.
> Let him take one of them, whichever he chooses,
> To Peleus' home, without paying a bride price.
>   (*Iliad*, Book 9, ll. 144–7: my translation)

Things are very different in fifth-century tragedy. From the surviving plays that tell of the avenging of Agamemnon's death, principally Aeschylus' *The Libation Bearers* (first performed in 458 B.C.) and the much later Electra plays by Sophocles and Euripides (the exact dates and even the relative chronology of the two plays are unknown),[4] we can piece together a story featuring not just Orestes, as in Homer, but also his companion Pylades and his sister Electra. This seems to have been shaped by poets of the seventh or sixth century and to have provided the essential background for the tragedians, though each of them had his own variations to play.

In outline the story went like this.[5] When Agamemnon was killed – in tragedy it is Clytemnestra who takes the leading role in the killing – the child Orestes was saved by being smuggled out of the palace, either by his nurse or by his elder sister Electra. He was taken to the northern land of Phocis, the area around Delphi, where King Strophius received him and brought him up along with his own son Pylades. When Orestes was grown up he consulted the oracle of Apollo at Delphi, which commanded him to take vengeance by stealth on the killers of his father. Electra meanwhile had been prevented from marrying, so as to avoid the possibility that a new generation of avengers might be born; she had remained in the family home, a constant reminder through her unceasing lamentation of the outrage that had been done to Agamemnon. When Orestes came back with Pylades to his native land, brother and sister were at first strangers to one another, but after they had met and recognised each other they took part together in a plot to kill Clytemnestra and Aegisthus. This entailed Orestes' gaining entry to the palace disguised as a traveller from Phocis and bringing news of his own supposed death. After the murders Orestes was driven mad by the pursuing Furies, but in the end was saved with Apollo's help. Electra was married to Pylades.

It was one of the essential features of this story that while her brother was in exile and the usurpers were in power Electra was kept unmarried, a wholly abnormal situation for a woman in ancient Greek society. Her very name, Elektra, was thought to refer to this abnormal status, recalling the adjective *alektros* ('without a marriage bed'). The etymology is unconvincing; but it was evidently familiar, to judge from an allusive bit of word play in Euripides,[6] and it probably goes back to one of the lost poems that influenced the tragedians. According to the scholar Aelian, writing many centuries later, the lyric poet Xanthus fitted Electra into the Homeric list of Agamemnon's daughters by explaining that Electra was originally called Laodice, 'but when Agamemnon was killed and Aegisthus married Clytemnestra and became king, as she was without a marriage bed and growing old in her virgin state the people of Argos called her Elektra, because she had no husband and no experience of a marriage bed'.[7] Along with the denial of marriage went physical maltreatment and deprivation in the usurpers' unnatural household, powerful images for the disorder created by the killing of the legitimate king. Euripides transposed Electra's home from the palace to a poor dwelling in the country, where though nominally married to a humble farmer she remained a virgin and suffered the material hardships of a peasant's life.

Another constant element in the story was the recognition of brother and sister. When Orestes returned, his first duty was to visit his father's tomb and to make offerings to the dead Agamemnon, including a lock of his own hair, which was duly found and recognised as his, whether by Electra or by some third party sympathetic to the cause of the avengers. The lyric poet Stesichorus[8] certainly used this motif of the lock as recognition token – his lost *Oresteia*, a long narrative poem in two books, was one of the main sources drawn upon by the tragedians – and we find all three dramatists using it, too, though Sophocles and Euripides do so with interesting variations. In Sophocles' play the lock is found and joyfully recognised by Chrysothemis, sister of Electra and Orestes, but Electra believes that Orestes is already dead and therefore dismisses its significance;[9] in Euripides there is a remarkable and notorious scene which seems to parody Aeschylus, with Electra scornfully (and, as it turns out, wrongly) rejecting the possibility that Orestes' hair could be matched with her own.[10] Evidently this was a motif that none of the tragedians wanted to dispense with; what it actually 'meant' is harder to establish, though the physical ties of kinship are one obvious theme, and the definition of identity is another. Both may be extremely problematic in a situation where children are preparing to kill one parent in the name of filial piety towards the other.

The next step in the story was the murder plot itself; in all our surviving versions from tragedy Electra has a share in the planning of the killings, as indeed does the audience, since in each case it is let into the secret shared by the avengers. In Aeschylus it is Orestes who takes the initiative and is the dominant partner, but both Sophocles and Euripides give more emphasis to Electra: Sophocles makes her 'stage-manage' the murder of Clytemnestra and use her mother's corpse as a trap for the unsuspecting Aegisthus,[11] while in Euripides it is she who devises the plan for the killing of her mother and actually helps to wield the sword.[12] This prominence, combined with the stress laid by both dramatists on the isolation and sexual deprivation of Electra, identifies her as a figure who challenges the gender boundaries of Greek society. We do not know how far their sources had already pointed in this direction, but it may well be right to see a sharpening of the focus on this issue in Sophocles and Euripides, with both of them bringing out the inherent contradiction in Electra's situation: it is precisely her need for female fulfilment that drives her beyond the bounds of approved feminine conduct. In Sophocles' version particular and ironic point is made of the fact that in her lamentation for her dead father, and later for her supposedly dead brother, Electra is fulfilling her role as close female relative with a duty to ensure that her dead kin are given proper ritual treatment.

The marriage to Pylades[13] seems not to have been a crucial part of the tragic scheme; there is no mention of Electra's future in Aeschylus or Sophocles, and even in Euripides the story is somewhat peripheral. The essence of Electra's situation seems to be that she is outside the ordinary categories of society. But she is not thereby rendered powerless; on the contrary, the very marginality of her position makes her deeply disturbing as soon as she starts taking the initiative.

Between them, the tragedians used the story of Electra to explore not only the contradictions of Electra's own situation but also the complex relations and disturbing similarities between mother and daughter (with more or less stress on the daughter's attachment to her dead father) and the interplay of feeling between brother and sister; Sophocles added the further complication of Electra's relations with her sister Chrysothemis, while Euripides introduced the new theme of the princess's 'marriage' to a humble farmer, which deprived her of status and power and the chance of becoming the mother of a royal avenger. Given all this richness it is not surprising that the story as dramatised in the fifth century B.C. has had a powerful continuing life in the literary imagination of the West.

Of all the aspects of the situation emphasised by the different dramatists, it was Aeschylus' treatment of the recognition scene that became a classic in the history of fifth-century theatre. This was evidently the highlight that inspired a series of vase paintings showing Electra with her urn at the tomb and the two young men in travelling dress;[14] and it may well have been the fame of this scene that influenced both Sophocles and Euripides in the choice of their own dramatic design. Aeschylus makes his Electra, under the guidance of the Chorus, turn the ritual of pouring drink-offerings to the dead Agamemnon, which Clytemnestra had commanded as a means of propitiating her victim, into a great prayer for vengeance on the murderers. This redirection of the ritual action is at once followed by Electra's discovery of a newly cut lock of hair on the tomb, to which she reacts with a mixture of intense hope and fear. A lock of hair could have been sent from abroad, but not footprints, which she now notices and tracks to their source, Orestes himself. For both Sophocles and Euripides it seems to have been important not to repeat the detail of this scene, and neither of them had Orestes and Electra meet at the tomb. But Electra with her urn remains a striking image. In Sophocles it is the urn handed to her by Orestes, supposedly containing Orestes' own ashes, over which she utters her most poignant laments;[15] and Euripides' play opens with Electra carrying an urn, though this one is neither a container for drink-offerings nor a funerary vessel, but a humble water pot which she is taking to the spring.[16] In both cases there seems to be some sort of play with the audience's expectations: what we are offered is not just a reworking of an old story, inherited from earlier poets, but a response, however ironic, to another famous tragedy. When Hofmannsthal and Strauss used Sophocles' *Electra* they were doing what Sophocles had himself done in relation to Aeschylus and possibly even in relation to Euripides.

The power of the Aeschylean model can best be seen in Electra's long speech in the recognition scene, which charts her response to the discovery of the lock and then the footprints. There is something almost operatic in this intense concentration on her fluctuating feelings:

(*Electra fears that the lock may not have been brought by Orestes himself, but could have been sent by someone on his behalf, perhaps after his death; and the Chorus echoes her anxiety*)

ELECTRA   I too feel a surge of bitter anger in my heart;
            I feel it like a piercing shaft.
            And from my eyes fall thirsty teardrops
            unrestrained, pouring in a dangerous flood
            as I look at this lock. How can I imagine
            that it belongs to someone else, one of the townspeople?
            Certainly it was not *she* who cut it from her head,
            the murderess, my mother, whose godless mind
            holds no motherly thoughts towards her children.
            No, this offering must belong to Orestes,
            dearest to me of mortal beings . . . I feel the touch of hope.
            Oh if only it had the power of speech, like a messenger!

Then I should not be torn by this uncertainty,
but either it would tell me plainly to throw this hair away
if the lock was cut from an enemy's head,
or as one of my kin it could share my lamentation
and adorn this tomb, to bring honour on my father.

We call on the gods, who know well
what tempests we are tossed in, like sailors at sea.
But if it is our destiny to win safety
a great tree could grow from a small seed.
Look! Footprints – a second token! . . .
                    (*The Libation Bearers*, ll. 183–205: my translation)

Whatever may have been true of earlier treatments of the story, by Aeschylus' time Electra has become vividly alive.

2 Hofmannsthal's 'Elektra': from Sophocles to Strauss

KAREN FORSYTH

I

In the autumn of 1901 Hugo von Hofmannsthal began the work that would lead into the long partnership with Richard Strauss. It would also be the first of their two operas based on Greek sources, the other being *Die ägyptische Helena* (1927). *Elektra* had a protracted genesis. Shortly before he started to work on it, Hofmannsthal was engaged on his tragedy *Pompilia*, the story of which he found in Robert Browning's *The Ring and the Book*. He approached the task carefully, even methodically. To Arthur Schnitzler he wrote (12 August 1901):

> In the mornings without exception I work on my big play with a lot of caution and consideration, quite differently from usual. For the first time in my life it is a really dramatic undertaking.[1]

There was the nub; Hofmannsthal was schooling himself in the drama. The previous year in his life had marked a personal and artistic crisis. He had originally been enrolled in the Faculty of Law at Vienna University, but now he was completing a doctorate entitled 'A Study of the Development of the Poet Victor Hugo' for the Faculty of Romance Philology. Yet he was deeply uncertain about pursuing an academic career, preferring to devote himself to writing. He withdrew to Paris to arm himself with plans against the future and also to think up practical ways of making money; for on 1 June 1901 he married Gerty Schlesinger,[2] and it would have been very foolish indeed to have hoped to support a family on poetry alone, poetry and verse dramas having comprised the main part of his œuvre to that date. It is clear from his letters to his parents from Paris that financial considerations played a good part in his interest in the stage, and he made no bones about regarding *Der Triumph der Zeit* (1900–1), the ballet he intended for Strauss, largely as a money-making enterprise.[3]

All through 1900 and 1901 Hofmannsthal planned, read, sketched or adapted plays. The first mention of *Elektra*, in a letter to his father, shows that it was initially viewed as a technical exercise to help in the writing of *Pompilia*:

> If only the weather would improve and I could see the countryside, which has been so overcast; and if my imagination were to loosen up in consequence, then I would like to start my adaptation of *Elektra*. It is hard to say why I should need such a change of weather in order to begin my tragedy with any zest or lightness of touch.[4]

Although *Pompilia* joined the large pile of Hofmannsthal's dramatic fragments,[5] it evidently encouraged him in his own work, because at the end of the year he withdrew his application for a teaching position at the University of Vienna. (This was the 'venia docendi'.) Work on *Elektra* did not progress at once. In June 1902 he told Theodor Gomperz of his plans for an unusual, two-part 'Oresteia', but there is no evidence that he had begun to write it. It was not until August 1903, when prompted by outward circumstances, that Hofmannsthal sat down to write *Elektra*, and then he wrote it in three weeks.

Of course the crisis of Hofmannsthal's middle and late twenties went a good deal deeper than matters of money or professional choice. Under the headings 'Preexistenz', Hofmannsthal's own abstract and unhelpful term, and 'Sprachkrise', referring to the 'Chandos Brief' (1902), different critical explanations have been offered.[6] Each surely contains something of the truth (if the truth of something so personal and so difficult is knowable), and the only excuse for adding a piece of speculation is that it may help to understand *Elektra*. Could it be that Hofmannsthal had forced himself into marriage and that his reasons for doing so were at the root of the problem? Compare the next two quotations, the first written twelve months after his marriage and the second two years later:

> [My thoughts about happiness are] connected with my deeper thoughts about marriage: that I value marriage in itself so highly and hold a very low opinion of this excessive talk about individual personalities, of whom it is claimed that only two in the whole world are meant for each other – who naturally never get each other. We are principally men and women, are children of parents and become parents of children, are entirely created to realize these *endless* relationships – we are also individual persons, but mostly negative and very seldom positive ones.[7]

> Friendship between men cannot form the content of life, but it is, I believe, the purest and strongest thing that life contains; for me, next to my natural vocation, it is the one thing I could not conceive of existing without, and I believe I would have sought it no matter what class I happened to be born into.[8]

Hofmannsthal was a practising Catholic[9] and the strictly and carefully-raised only son of devoted parents. He was also a devoted letter-writer, and the bulk of his correspondence was addressed to male friends. Poetry had been the product of his youth, and youth had been a time for Hofmannsthal when male friendship might and did form the content of life – though there were a few intimate friendships with women as well. On 14 February 1902, shortly after his twenty-eighth birthday, he wrote to Rudolf Alexander Schröder:

It was my twenty-eighth birthday, and I believe I can understand as follows the alarming paralysis of my productive powers which has been going on for nearly two years – with certain deceptive interruptions: it is the painful transition from the productivity of youth to that of manhood, a deep inward process of transformation, felt outwardly only through grief and dullness.[10]

It is not surprising, then, to find Hofmannsthal in the early years of his marriage restless and unsettled. Neither is it surprising, given his firm notion of duty and social responsibility,[11] that he could not write poetry. He turned to drama because it was less personal. But how very early he put his finger on the weakness that would dog all his output for the stage:

Just how far, given my way of seeing the world, one can after all see conflicts, or rather, as drama demands, the concentration of an entire existence into one final conflict – that is what I hope to show you and other friends more clearly and richly than I could in words through the dramatic products that are tentatively taking shape in me.[12]

Luckily for him, an adaptation of *Elektra* without dramatic conflict was almost unthinkable. Doubly lucky perhaps that in the end he was obliged to write it so fast; he tampered little with the plot and dramatic construction, and let the power and originality of his language bear the burden of carrying us back to Sophocles.

II

The circumstances of the adaptation are clearly set out in a letter to Otto Brahm. In May 1903 Hofmannsthal met the producer Max Reinhardt and the actress Gertrud Eysoldt at Hermann Bahr's house. Hofmannsthal had just seen Eysoldt in Gorky's play *The Lower Depths*[13] and had been very impressed. He mentioned his vague plans for an 'Elektra' to them, and these were immediately seized upon with a view to a production at Reinhardt's Kleines Theater in Berlin, with Eysoldt in the title role, in October or December of that year. The adaptation was in this sense an occasional piece, with

Eysoldt's interpretation of the leading role in *The Lower Depths*
encouraging Hofmannsthal to a certain full-blooded theatricality.[14]
The première took place on 30 October 1903.

Although *Elektra* was the first play Hofmannsthal had finished in
four years, he was never entirely pleased with it; he had evidently
written it in an uncertain frame of mind, had unspecified reservations about its construction, found its atmosphere too black and
considered its success unmerited. Nevertheless the play was a phe-
nomenal overnight success:

We have had what people call a great success: a long series of productions is
to be expected, the play accepted by 22 theatres in the first 4 days, three
impressions of the book sold out, a great brouhaha in the press.[15]

Readers, audiences and critics alike have continued to be stunned
by the violence and extremity of emotion in Hofmannsthal's *Elektra*,
by its vehemence and excess, and by the apparent modernity of its
psychological premises. Critics have drawn attention to Rohde,
Bachofen, Bahr and most particularly to Freud.[16] *Elektra* is spoken
of as a study of a psyche *in extremis* and as a psychoanalytic
drama.[17] Very few critics, however, have actually troubled to read
and compare Hofmannsthal with the Greek sources, and only one,
to my knowledge, has given the original sources their due.[18] Obviously Hofmannsthal was influenced by contemporary thought. But
the originality of the ideas current in Vienna at the turn of the century should not be overestimated, and few people were less likely to
make this mistake than Hofmannsthal. Furthermore, a distinct line
must be drawn for critical purposes between that which was 'in the
air' in 1903 and that which Hofmannsthal actually read. For example, he may not have read Breuer's and Freud's *Studien über Hysterie*
(1895), often cited as being central to his *Elektra*, until at least
1904.[19] In any case *Hamlet* is arguably the most important 'secondary' source for *Elektra*.[20]

Hofmannsthal probably knew all three ancient versions of the
Electra myth. There is internal evidence that he knew Aeschylus' *The
Libation Bearers*. There is no evidence, internal or external, that he
had read the *Electra* of Euripides – but it seems improbable that a
man so well-read should not have done, or have seen it performed
at the theatre. However, the main source and the main influence on
Hofmannsthal was Sophocles' *Electra*. This cannot be stressed often
enough, and Hofmannsthal's subtitle 'Tragödie in einem Aufzug
frei nach Sophokles' ('Tragedy in One Act Freely Adapted from
Sophocles') makes it plain. A note of 1903 is revealing:

I have not touched the figures. I have only rearranged the cloak of words which hung around their bronze existences, so that advocacy is put into the shade and poetry is brought into the light.[21]

Who then is Sophocles' Electra? She is a woman who bears the consequences of exceptional love and exceptional hatred. Many years after Agamemnon's death she still grieves bitterly each day at dawn[22] as if the murder had taken place yesterday. Her affection also extends to her brother, whom she courageously rescued from Clytemnestra and in whose return she rejoices. She has a strong sense of family honour and a well-developed concept of royalty (both are part of her Greekness). She is intelligent, articulate, unselfish and brave enough to contemplate taking extreme action. Both her memory and her will-power are strong and reinforce one another. These are her admirable qualities.

At the same time she feels violent and bitter hatred for those who have perpetrated the murder and for their associates. She resents having had to suffer and to sacrifice any chance of motherhood. She is mocking, abusive, sarcastic, taunting, ironical and shockingly explicit. She is capable of dissembling (as when she leads Aegisthus to his death) and of callous and bloodthirsty enjoyment of revenge. Nothing could surpass in venom her cry of 'Strike her again, strike!' (l. 1415)[23] as Orestes murders Clytemnestra. Socially debased and physically maltreated, forced to dress in rags and eat like a beggar, she is outraged by the moral weakness and putrefaction of those about her, whose complicity with Aegisthus she despises. The tragic paradox of her case is that she loathes human bestiality and yet is brought to apparent bestiality herself. But such is the stress of her situation. She is, as she says, 'beside herself' (l. 223). As Hofmannsthal remarked of tragic characters in general, she goes down to the regions of hell.[24]

Hofmannsthal claims truly that he did not touch the figures. His Elektra is Sophocles' in almost all respects, down to small details and borrowed lines and phrases too numerous to mention.[25] He was interested in this character both because he understood her psychology and also, it must be said, from a literary point of view: such a literary man as Hofmannsthal could not fail to draw a comparison between Sophocles' play and that great model of German Classicism, Goethe's *Iphigenie*, whose bloodless sublimity and calm dignity had provoked Goethe's own epithet 'verteufelt human', and which was in every way the opposite of *Electra*. Hofmannsthal clearly hoped to revitalise myth with the blood of Electra:

Cortina. – Defence of Elektra – devilishly humane – The differences are enormous. There the gigantic space. Here the nutshell . . . There the chorus that sang like the roaring of the surf. The figures enlarged. A single stretching of an arm infinitely meaningful. The horror of the myth blowing across with the wind off the sea, hanging above in the clouds. We must create the horror of myth *anew* for ourselves. Let shadows emerge again from the blood. Figures in Goethe's Iphigenie are only lightly immersed in their fate. Experience is only a simile. How completely alien tragedy was to Goethe.[26]

None of the characters in Hofmannsthal's *Elektra* could be described as being 'only lightly immersed in their fate'. Klytämnestra, like Clytemnestra, is villainous yet troubled. Sophocles' queen lies 'by day or night denied the cloak of sleep' (l. 781). And she is troubled by dreams (l. 438). Hofmannsthal develops this into rotting superstition. Klytämnestra turns pathetically to Elektra as a drowning woman to a rock:

KLYTÄMNESTRA   Du redest
              von alten Dingen so, wie wenn sie gestern
              geschehen wären. Aber ich bin morsch.
              Ich denke, aber alles türmt sich mir
              eins übers andre. (p. 202)[27]

              You speak / of things past as if they /
              had happened yesterday. But I am
              rotten. / I think, but everything rises up
              in me in confusion.

Elektra, opening with irony and double meaning, like Hamlet, who 'sets up a glass' to his mother's inmost self, then shows Klytämnestra her own soul.

Chrysothemis in both Sophocles and Hofmannsthal is the weaker sister, wanting motherhood and an easier time of it. Aegisthus is presented as cowardly and womanish in both. Orestes in both is merely the agent of revenge.

But although Hofmannsthal keeps to the essentials of Sophocles' characters and plot, there *are* some differences, the most obvious one being that at the end of his play Hofmannsthal's Elektra collapses and dies.[28] With her death can be linked most of the ideas behind the original contribution which Hofmannsthal made in this adaptation. The ideas are complicated, needless to say, and fortunately there is another note of 1903 that helps in the business of untangling them:

The repetitions, digressions and pragmatic passages of the ancient text may give pleasure to an audience absorbed in the subject-matter and may be mitigated by rhythmic and musical embellishments. I am not unappreciative of the splendour of a passage like the following (Elektra lamenting over the dead Orestes, with the Chorus). For us familiarity with the myth is a great advantage. We can handle the figures as we would angels or the devil, Cinderella or the wicked stepmother. We can direct all our attention to that which lies outside of the pragmatic part, to the storm clouds gathered above the mountains: to that 'die and live again!' in the mystic belief in suffering and doing, Maeterlinck's world . . . But in all this I am guided by my feeling.[29]

It is a naive lapse to suggest that an ancient audience was less familiar with its myths than we are with, for example, Cinderella. Other aspects of his line of thought are more seriously mistaken.

To the ancient Greeks, Electra's and Orestes' fate at the end of the play indicated to what extent theirs was an act of justifiable matricide. Electra's death would be taken as a condemnation of her life. The outcome of the play is intimately bound up with the moral arguments for and against the conduct of the members of the House of Atreus, arguments which Hofmannsthal refers to as passages of 'advocacy' or 'pragmatism'. In neither Aeschylus nor Euripides nor Sophocles do Electra and Orestes die. In *The Eumenides* Orestes is pursued by the Furies, seeks sanctuary at Delphi and goes to the Areopagus at Athens, where he is acquitted and granted absolution. In Euripides Electra (previously married to a peasant) is given in marriage to Pylades, hardly her equal but 'a good man'. Orestes is pursued by the Furies to Athens, as in Aeschylus, and is acquitted. Apollo assumes the blame. Sophocles passes briefer judgment:

> Now for the House of Atreus
> Freedom is won
> From all her suffering,
> And this day's work well done. (Sophocles, *Electra*, ll. 1507–10)

That there are variants to the ending shows how important it was.

Hofmannsthal thought he could separate Elektra's death from the moral argument of the myth. There are two passages in Sophocles that may have prompted him to imagine Elektra's death. Early in the play Electra addresses the Chorus:

> I am beside myself,
> I know. Terrors too strong
> Have driven me down. And now
> This passion can have no end
> Till my life ends. What use is there
> In comfortable words?
> Leave me alone,
> Kind sisters, there is no escape
> From this. My sum of woe
> Outruns all reckoning. (Sophocles, *Electra*, ll. 223–32)

But at the time of saying this she is convinced that all is lost and that

Orestes will never come. ('Half my life is wasted in hopeless waiting' (ll. 182–3).) It can be read as an expression of profound despair. Later, on hearing the lie of Orestes' accident at the Pythian Games, she says: 'Life is all pain to me: I want to die', and sinks to the ground. It might also be suggested that her willingness to commit the murders alone (ll. 1041–2) implies a suicidal readiness for death.

However, although perhaps initially prompted by these lines of Sophocles, Hofmannsthal was mainly swayed by his own, not entirely watertight, theories on the nature of individual identity and action. (Whether he was also swayed by a desire to give Gertrud Eysoldt a strong final curtain must remain an open question.) In 'Ad me ipsum', his own interpretation of his work, he describes three ways of leaving 'Preexistenz' and joining 'das Soziale':

The path to society as the path to the higher self: the non-mystic way.

(a)   through action
(b)   through work
(c)   through children

If a person leaves that totality (pre-existence, being without fate) then he is in danger of losing himself, of going astray: he looks for that which belongs to him, the deciding factor, the equivalent: in the 'Abenteurer' the solution is ironically suggested (work and children).
a) transformation through action. To act is to relinquish the self. The Alcestis – and Oedipus – theme sublimated in the 'Elektra'. (The relationship of Elektra to action admittedly treated with irony. Elektra – Hamlet.) The decisive factor is not action but fidelity.[30]

To say that to act means to sacrifice one's individuality is a piece of sophistry. But what about the ironic relationship of Elektra to action and the comparison with Hamlet? Elektra does not vacillate, unlike Hamlet; she never ceases to will the action, unlike Hamlet; and her attitude to action is not ironic, unlike Hamlet's. Taking the play overall, it is quite clear that Elektra is unflinching in her fidelity. Given the constraints of sex, which are not at issue, we accept this fidelity in place of action and can agree with Hofmannsthal when he says: 'The decisive factor is not action but fidelity.' The Hamlet comparison may refer to Elektra's failure to give her brother the axe (the weapon used against Agamemnon, which she has been keeping). There are many references to the axe early in the play, and Hofmannsthal makes much of it in the final scene before Orestes goes into the house. Yet he presents it as *more* than just an ironic outward and physical failure, if this is the kind of irony he alludes to in the quotation above:

ELEKTRA   . . . nur der ist selig,
       der seine Tat zu tuen kommt! und selig,
       wer ihn anrühren darf, und wer das Beil
       ihm aus der Erde gräbt, und wer die Fackel
       ihm hält, und wer die Tür ihm auftut . . . (p. 229)
       . . . he alone is blessed / who comes to perform
       his deed! and blessed / is he who may touch him,
       and who digs / the axe out of the ground for him,
       and who holds / the torch for him, and who opens
       the door for him . . .

But she is unable to give him the axe:

       Ich habe ihm das Beil nicht geben können!
       Sie sind gegangen, und ich habe ihm
       das Beil nicht geben können. Es sind keine
       Götter im Himmel! (p. 229)

       I could not give him the axe! / They have left and
       I could not / give him the axe. There are no / gods
       in heaven!

We sense that we are supposed to see this as a deep-seated Hamlet-like neurosis. But this does not fit with the heroically resolute Elektra of 'Nun denn allein', nor with the way she conducts Aegisthus to his death, nor with her lines to Klytämnestra when she anticipates her mother's death:

ELEKTRA   . . . sausend fällt das Beil,
       und ich steh da und seh dich endlich sterben!
       Dann träumst du nimmermehr, dann brauche ich
       nicht mehr zu träumen, und wer dann noch lebt,
       der jauchzt und kann sich seines Lebens freuen! (p. 210)

       . . . the axe falls with a rushing sound, / and
       I stand there and see you die at last! / Then you
       will never dream again, then I will / not need to
       dream, and whoever is still alive / rejoices and
       can enjoy life!

The axe episode is a minor and unsuccessful detail; the comparison with Hamlet partially valid. But the question of Elektra's death is less easily passed by. Her final words do not provide much help:

ELEKTRA   Schweig und tanze. Alle müssen
       herbei! hier schliesst euch an! Ich trag die Last
       des Glückes, und ich tanze vor euch her.
       Wer glücklich ist wie wir, dem ziehmt nur eins:
       schweigen und tanzen! (pp. 233–4)

       Be silent and dance. Everyone must / come!
       Join on here! I bear / the burden of happiness,

and I dance ahead of you. / Whoever is happy
as we are can do only one thing: / be silent
and dance.

Having fulfilled her task, she is supposed not to have anything
more to live for, so completely does she identify with the deed. Hofmannsthal expresses the idea in another way in a note of 1905:

In 'Elektra' an individual is cancelled out in an empirical way when the con-
tents of her life are shattered from within, in the same way that water turning
to ice shatters an earthenware jug. Elektra is no longer Elektra because she
dedicated herself entirely to being Elektra.[31]

In *Elektra* Hofmannsthal clearly thought he could separate
psychology and poetical substance from the circumstances and
sources of dramatic conflict: 'We can direct all our attention to that
which lies outside of the pragmatic part, to the storm clouds
gathered above the mountains . . .' But life does not hang like clouds
above a range of mountains; at least, in good drama, the mountains
and the sky above are one. Indeed with Elektra's death and the complex of ideas related to action and individuality, to 'that "die and live
again!" in the mystic belief in suffering and doing', Hofmannsthal
had begun to push quite a different range of mountains under his
storm. But since he had until that point worked closely from a well-
known myth grounded in moral conflict, his ending must seem
poetic rather than dramatic.

This same tendency to abstract a psychological and poetical
play from the stuff of the plot determined the other changes Hofmannsthal made. Orestes' part is cut to a minimum: Hofmannsthal
even agreed with the critic who suggested that it would have been
better if Orestes had not appeared at all.[32] But it must be said that
there are aspects of this part which a modern audience might find
digressive, such as the long account of the Pythian Games, or alien,
such as the attention given to libations and other religious obser-
vances, or too slow, such as the long build-up to the recognition; Hofmannsthal had good reasons to cut these. He also cut Clytemnestra's
speech of self-defence (Sophocles, *Electra*, ll. 515–40) concerning
Agamemnon's sacrifice of Iphigenia, drastically compressed in
Sophocles already as compared to Aeschylus and Euripides. This
was less defensible; conflict is diminished if Clytemnestra is completely black. Furthermore Hofmannsthal cut the time spent on the
double murder, perhaps thinking that a modern audience might not
relish violence in quite Sophocles' long-drawn-out way. Much more
importantly, he cut the Chorus. A Chorus upon a modern stage is
awkward, even unthinkable. But Hofmannsthal removed both the
Chorus and its voice, that great rational, humane and moderating

force within the play, which was in every sense a pragmatic presence. Elektra's psychological state is made *less* rather than more tragic or plausible by the absence of the Chorus, the more so because the Chorus is also the institution of rational dialogue, ensuring at least a level of rational contact between the protagonists. Nothing could be more effective than the following exchange between Electra and Clytemnestra:

ELECTRA   I kept [Orestes] alive,
           You have often said, to be your executioner.
           Yes, if I could, I would have done just that,
           I tell you to your face. Denounce me for it,
           Denounce me in public, call me what you will –
           Vile, brutal, shameless – if I am all these,
           I am your true daughter!
CHORUS   She is angry now,
           And little concerned with justice, if you ask me.
CLYTEMNESTRA I've reason to be concerned with her, I think,
           If this is the language she uses to her mother.
           And she a grown woman. Is there anything
           She will not stoop to? She has no shame at all.
ELECTRA   I *am* ashamed, believe me, for what I have said;
           You may not think it, but I am ashamed
           Of my rudeness and ill-temper. It is you,
           Your hatred and ill-treatment drive me on
           To act against my nature; villainy
           Is taught by vile example.
                         (Sophocles, *Electra*, ll. 601–19)

In the whole of Hofmannsthal's adaptation there is no dialogue so dramatic, because there is never so much conflict within one person. Sophocles' passion within rationality has greater dramatic range than Hofmannsthal's pure feeling.

In the poetic bias of his adaptation Hofmannsthal in fact reveals his far deeper natural affinity with Aeschylus than with Sophocles. The diction, imagery and symbolism of the whole work have the flavour of Aeschylus, but it is most evident in the extended blood imagery of Elektra's great opening monologue.[33] Each day at dusk Elektra observes an hour of ritual mourning for her father. Filial devotion, murder, revenge and royalty are her themes, all united by blood: blood relationship, bloody murder and revenge, royal blood. Blood flows, spurts, streams and gushes through her speech to the final vision of the blood sacrifice and the dance:

ELEKTRA Von den Sternen
         stürzt alle Zeit herab, so wird das Blut
         aus hundert Kehlen stürzen auf dein Grab! (p. 191)

>All time spurts down from the stars; so
>will / blood from a hundred throats spurt
>onto your grave!

This vision then imitates the movement of unstoppable blood in an extraordinary sentence of thirty lines (p. 191). There is no exact parallel in Aeschylus, but he speaks of 'vengeful gore', 'blood rain', 'blood guilt' and 'streaming blood'.[34] Clytemnestra uses a most striking image to describe Agamemnon's dying moments:

CLYTEMNESTRA   Thus he went down and the life struggled out of him;
And as he died he spattered me with the dark red
And violent driven rain of bitter savoured blood
To make me glad, as gardens stand among the showers
Of God in glory at the birthtime of the buds.

(ll. 1390–4)

Hofmannsthal wished the blood imagery to be the pervasive image in his play, and carried it through into the exclusively black and red décor of his stage setting.

III

Hofmannsthal's language has much that can bear comparison with Aeschylus in strength and vividness, and this must have been an attraction for Strauss. In 1903 Strauss may possibly have seen the Berlin première.[35] But it was not until 1906[36] that the idea of making an opera was raised. From a letter to Gertrud Eysoldt it is clear that Hofmannsthal was in Berlin from 20 to 23 November 1905 (to cast *Ödipus und die Sphinx* with Max Reinhardt).[37] Strauss was at this time conductor of the Berlin Court Opera and Principal Conductor of the Berlin Philharmonic Orchestra. It seems highly likely that Strauss and Hofmannsthal met in November 1905. The first mention of *Elektra* in the Strauss–Hofmannsthal correspondence is on 7 March 1906, in terms that would fit with a November meeting. In a later letter Hofmannsthal refers to a Berlin meeting.[38]

At this meeting it was evidently agreed that Strauss should have a free hand in cutting the stage play and in this way making a libretto (as he had done with *Salome*). For Hofmannsthal it began as a business arrangement:

I, as well as my publisher, will renounce in favour of your music publisher all our rights in the libretto for *Elektra* as shortened by you and thus distinguished from the play, in return for a royalty in the German as well as in all foreign editions of this libretto to be settled between the publishers.[39]

There have been many assessments of the Strauss–Hofmannsthal collaboration. No doubt at the beginning, and quite legitimately, Hofmannsthal, who was not yet financially secure, entered the partnership for financial gain. The recent success of *Salome* made Strauss look like a very good bet indeed. Writing to his father in 1907 (on the benefits of travel to Germany), Hofmannsthal made his hopes quite plain: 'If (as I hope from the relationship with Strauss) a situation should arise such that I can ignore material concerns (and I don't ask for better), then everything is really all right.'[40] There is circumstantial evidence that Hofmannsthal initially held himself to be the superior talent and that he gradually reversed his opinion, though this must be read between the lines. However, he never gave Strauss less than his best, and so it was in the few extra passages he provided for *Elektra*.

Sophocles' play is 1,510 lines long; Hofmannsthal's stage adaptation is about the same length. The libretto is approximately 825 lines long, and this includes the three new passages written by Hofmannsthal. As a general rule Strauss cut the text where it was too wordy to make a good libretto. He did not cut in order to change Hofmannsthal's interpretation: he cut to make it shorter.

Some cuts were suggested by Hofmannsthal. In a letter of 18 July 1906 Hofmannsthal noted that the brief interlude between the Cook and the Young Servant was superfluous. In a style which is a mixture of Viennese humour and Shakespeare's comic servants, the Young Servant repeats the news so recently and so tragically delivered. Comic repetition provides emotional release. After a long preamble he concludes:

> Und kurz und gut: der junge Bursch Orest,
> der Sohn vom Haus, der immer ausser Haus war
> und drum so gut wie tot: kurz dieser, der
> schon eh und immer sozusagen tot war,
> der ist nun sozusagen wirklich tot! (p. 213)

> And in a word: that young lad Orestes, / the son of the
> house, who was always away from home / and so as good
> as dead: in a word, this clap, who / for ages was as good as
> dead, / is now so to speak really dead!

Clearly this is too verbose for a libretto. But Strauss with his sixth sense for the stage knew that a comic interlude, however brief, would be effective at this point. He shortened the scene and removed the Cook, but did not cut it entirely.

In the same letter Hofmannsthal proposed that Orestes should be recognised not by one but by up to twenty-four old servants. Evidently there had been a conversation about introducing another

chorus in addition to the servant girls. But Hofmannsthal's suggestion, if badly directed, could look ridiculous, and in the end the score
and libretto had three accompanying servants.

On 22 December 1907 Strauss wrote to Hofmannsthal about the
double murder. In conversation Hofmannsthal must have suggested
leaving Aegisthus out altogether, in keeping with his tendency to
simplify. Strauss knew better. What bothered him was the amount of
running on and off done by the women servants. He suggested that it
would be better to have the murders done in the house at the same
time. On 3 January 1908 Hofmannsthal sent detailed proposals of
how to do this, but in the end it was left exactly as Hofmannsthal
originally wrote it. Although this may look awkward on paper, in
practice it works well enough.

Hofmannsthal wrote new lines for two episodes in the opera: the
recognition scene and the Elektra–Chrysothemis duet after the
murders. Both editions of Hofmannsthal's collected works[41] incor-
rectly give a third passage as being new. This is the twelve-line addition to Elektra's speech to Klytämnestra describing her mother's
death:

> Hinab die Treppe durch Gewölbe hin,
> Gewölbe nach Gewölbe geht die Jagd –
> und ich! ich! ich, die ihn dir geschickt,
> ich bin wie ein Hund an deiner Ferse,
> willst du in eine Höhle, spring ich dich
> von seitwärts an, so treiben wir dich fort –
> bis eine Mauer alles sperrt und dort
> im tiefsten Dunkel, doch ich seh ihn wohl,
> ein Schatten und doch Glieder und das Weisse
> von einem Auge doch, da sitzt der Vater:
> er achtet's nicht und doch muss es geschehen:
> zu seinen Füssen drücken wir dich hin . . . (p. 237)

> Down the stairs through vaults, / through vault after
> vault goes the hunt – / and I, I, I, who sent him to you, /
> I am like a dog at your heels, / if you try to get into a
> cave I spring at you / from the side, so we drive you
> away – / until a wall bars everything and there / in
> deepest darkness, yet I see him well, / a shadow and
> yet limbs and the white / of an eye, there father sits: /
> he isn't aware of it and yet it must happen: / we force
> you down at his feet . . .

In fact these lines occur in Elektra's speech to Chrysothemis (pp.
197–8) and have been adroitly transposed by Strauss. The metaphor
of the hunt (with Orestes as huntsman) provides the point of connection. Strauss had only to change from the third person pronoun to
the second. This is the only instance where Strauss transposes lines

from speeches in different scenes (some lines are transposed from adjacent speeches), and presumably it was done to avoid Hofmannsthal's ten-line description of the reaction of the gods, who had otherwise been scarcely mentioned.

On the two occasions when Strauss did ask for extra lines it was because the emotional climaxes in the play had been handled relatively tersely. In the play, when Elektra at last recognises Orestes, all she says before rejecting his embrace is:

ELEKTRA (*ganz leise, behand*)   Orest!
          Es rührt sich niemand. O lass deine Augen
          mich sehen! (p. 225)

          (*very softly, trembling*) Orestes! / Nobody
          is stirring. Oh let your eyes / look upon me!

But Strauss wanted this moment to be a lyrical climax and a point of repose. Hofmannsthal provided an extra nine lines in a tender vein.[42] Similarly, after the murders and before Elektra's dance Strauss wanted a simultaneous duet for Elektra and Chrysothemis. The words that Hofmannsthal supplied for the duet are the weakest in the libretto. They seem to hint at a 'Liebestod' for Elektra and end with the cryptic lines:

ELEKTRA (*feurig*) Ai! Liebe tötet! aber keiner fährt dahin
          und hat die Liebe nicht gekannt! (p. 239)

          (*passionately*) Ah! Love kills! / but nobody
          passes on / without having known love!

Hofmannsthal would clearly have preferred to leave Elektra to her silent dance.

Apart from a few small weaknesses, such as the above,[43] *Elektra* made a libretto of unrivalled quality. With what interest Hofmannsthal must have waited to hear how his words would sound in Strauss's setting. This was a new experience for him; nothing of his had previously been set to music. On 11 December 1906 he wrote to his father:

Today Richard Strauss played and sang large parts of 'Elektra' for me. It is *very* beautiful, and the poetry gains rather than loses.[44]

On the following day he wrote to Helene von Nostitz, again in glowing terms. Strauss had certainly not composed the whole opera, but even by then Hofmannsthal rated the opera higher than he rated his own stage adaptation:

Yesterday Richard Strauss played and sang for me several sections of 'Elektra', and the words in this form (although of course he sings dreadfully) gave me great pleasure, much more than when spoken by actors. So far as I can judge, he has done a tremendous job of contrasting the figure of 'Elektra' with her more gentle sister. I think that it will become very beautiful.[45]

More than a year later, on 27 February 1908, Hofmannsthal commented neutrally to his father that Strauss had played him a lot of *Elektra*.[46] The première was not until the following year, six years after Hofmannsthal had written his play. Not surprisingly, he felt extremely detached from the work by then. It was for this reason and no other that the Berlin and Dresden premières left him cold.[47] Gradually, after seeing these performances and assisting at rehearsals, he warmed to the work again, and there is no reason to believe that he changed his early, favourable opinion of Strauss's music.

3 The music of 'Elektra': some preliminary thoughts

I

Three of the changes Strauss made to Hofmannsthal's play (or that Hofmannsthal made at his request) are of special interest from a musical point of view. The first involves the insertion of Agamemnon's name at four key points in Elektra's monologue. In the play he is referred to here simply as 'Vater'; indeed his name is not mentioned at all until the recognition scene, just before the moment when Elektra identifies herself to her brother.[1] This of course was deliberate on Hofmannsthal's part.[2] However, there were good reasons for introducing the name at this point. It furnished essential information for those who did not know who Elektra's father was (for a similar reason Strauss added the phrase 'Tochter Klytämnestras' after 'Tochter meiner Mutter' in the next scene); it identified the leitmotive sounding in the orchestra at the same time (just as the mother's name would identify *her* leitmotive later); and, perhaps most important, it provided a means of formal articulation. Reducing the monologue to Elektra's cries of 'Agamemnon!' and 'Vater!' creates the following scheme:

> [2 lines]
> Agamemnon! Agamemnon!
> [18 lines]
> Agamemnon! Vater!
> [3 lines]
> Vater! Agamemnon!
> [30 lines]
> Agamemnon! Agamemnon!

The symmetry is obvious: Strauss frames the monologue with two double statements of 'Agamemnon!' (the opening couplet is more of an introduction than part of the monologue proper), adding two single statements around the mid-point. The father's name becomes a structural refrain.[3]

33

Secondly, Strauss made major changes in Chrysothemis' main speech.[4] In Hofmannsthal the sequence of ideas is as follows:[5]

(1) In my breast there is a burning fire that sends me wandering round the house.
(2) Were it not for you [Elektra], they would let us go.
(3) I want to have children.
(4) Our father is dead. Our brother does not come back.
(5) One day after another engraves its passing with a knife in your face and mine . . . and women whom I have known slender are heavy with blessings, drag themselves to the well . . . and out of them themselves flows sweet drink, and a living creature clings to them, sucking, and the children grow big –
(6) And for ever we sit like caged birds . . . and no one comes – no brother, no messenger from the brother, no messenger from a messenger, nothing!
(7) Much better be dead than be alive and not live.
(8) No, I am a woman and I want a woman's lot.

In the libretto, nos. 1–4 are in the same order, but 5–8 have been rearranged: the order is (6), (5), (8), (7). In other words, Strauss has put similar thoughts together ('Our father is dead, our brother does not come back, and for ever we sit like caged birds') and let the rhetoric build to a climax ('the children grow big – no, I am a woman and I want a woman's lot'), while at the same time keeping the throwaway line ('much better be dead') as an afterthought.[6] The result is a more conventional sequence of ideas than before; Chrysothemis seems less incoherent. But Strauss now has a clear-cut musical form. After the introductory (1) and (2), (3) presents the main thematic idea (four bars after Fig. 86); (4), (6) and (5) provide a middle section; and (8) allows a reprise of (3), with (7) acting as coda. Tonally, of course, the piece is a rondo, establishing E flat as tonic in (1), returning to it in (3) and finally reaffirming it, after excursions to remote regions, in (8), the whole capped with a strong V–I cadence (on *Weiberschicksal*, 'woman's lot', Fig. 109). But whether the piece is viewed formally or tonally it is obvious that Strauss has created a closed structure; the cadence is especially striking.

The third example, from the recognition scene, again shows him creating a closed structure, not through the transposition of lines, however, this time, but through the addition of new ones. The nine lines[7] Hofmannsthal added at Strauss's request[8] became the basis of a self-contained aria, complete with V–I cadence at the end (Figs. 149a–53a). It even cadences on the dominant halfway through. (Thus the most sustained melodic statement in the opera was actually based on an interpolation.)[9]

Other changes, such as those in the Klytämnestra scene, are more complex, and their musical consequences less clear. But the general tendency seems to be to clarify, to break down the structure into units, to establish symmetries. This is perhaps a natural response in a composer faced with a continuous, one-act text;[10] Strauss even goes so far as to divide the opera into mutually reflecting halves, as is evidenced by the fact that he starts a second series of rehearsal numbers (with 1a) at the mid-point. Hofmannsthal's play is already rather sectional and episodic; Strauss emphasises this feature in his setting. More on this topic below.

For the moment I want to go back to the Agamemnon motive, and Strauss's apparent need to identify it by name. In my chapter on *Salome* as a music drama, in the Cambridge Opera Handbook devoted to that work, I make the point that Strauss's conception of the leitmotive (as opposed to his actual practice) was a simplistic one, which he inherited from Wagner reception of the time. He really seems to have thought in terms of short, sharply characterised motives, each with a fixed dramatic connotation. This is borne out by the sketches. Those for *Elektra* – at least, those that have been published – almost have the character of a leitmotive guide.[11] On the very first page[12] (see Plate 2) we find musical ideas under the headings 'Das Schicksal der Atriden' ('the fate of the house of Atreus'),[13] 'Agamemnon' (the Agamemnon motive as it appears at the beginning of the score), 'Elektras Hass' ('Elektra's hatred', not the motive as it appears in her monologue but an early version of it), 'Das Geschick der Atriden' (a variant of the first motive listed) and 'Die Katze' (an idea for the maids' scene). In the case of the Agamemnon motive Strauss actually writes the name over the notes, leaving no doubt as to the meaning the motive had for him. That it is capable of being given a different interpretation is shown by Carolyn Abbate below.[14] The point here is simply that Strauss's clear-cut conception of the motive (which is bound up with his need to introduce the name 'Agamemnon' into the score at the moment when the motive sounds), coupled with his desire to clarify the dramatic structure at every point, produces a kind of music drama very different from Wagner's.

II

One of the attractions for Strauss of Hofmannsthal's play, along with the opportunities it offered for characterisation (especially the contrasts between the three principal women), was 'the tremendous

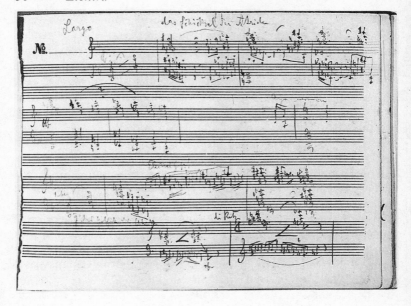

2: The first page of Strauss's sketches for *Elektra*, Sketchbook 17, folio 1
(see p. 35)

increase in musical tension to the very end', the famous *crescendo*
effect which sometimes gives the impression that *Elektra* consists of
one climax after another.[15] How does this square with the symmetrical, two-part form mentioned above?

The sectional nature of the play, with its stagey series of dialogues
(not to mention the old-fashioned, sub-Shakespearian effect of the
monologue immediately following the maids' scene), is clear enough:

(1)   The maids
(2)   Elektra
(3)   Elektra and Chrysothemis
(4)   Elektra and Klytämnestra
(5)   Elektra and Chrysothemis (with an 'interlude' for two servants)
(6)   Elektra and Orestes
(7)   Finale: the murders, Elektra's dance and death[16]

This has inevitably prompted comparisons with the symphonic
poem; Overhoff even analyses the work in terms of sonata form.[17]
Whatever we may think of such ideas (and Arnold Whittall discusses
them further below), the symmetry is unmistakable. For conve-

nience's sake Strauss begins his renumbering with Scene 5, which is also preceded by a double-barline;[18] but the work plainly hinges on the Klytämnestra scene, the longest scene in the opera and the dramatic turning-point. Around this keystone, everything goes by pairs (as Strauss said of *Capriccio*):[19] the two Chrysothemis scenes on either side, the monologue which has its counterpart in the finale (it is musically recapitulated there). Only the scene with Orestes, which could obviously have no counterpart, and the scene with the maids, which is customarily regarded as a prelude or prologue, stand outside of this scheme.

Such are the dramatic parallels between the two halves. Apart from his rehearsal-numbering, however, Strauss makes little obvious attempt to carry these parallels into the music (deeper correspondences are discussed by Tethys Carpenter below). At the beginning of Scene 5 it seems as if a large-scale recapitulation is to begin: the music returns to a key signature of one flat, as in Scene 1, and there are thematic references both to this scene and to the earlier scene with Chrysothemis. The parallels are not continued, however,[20] since the advent of Orestes necessarily involves the introduction of new thematic material (not to mention the servants' interlude, an extended anticipation of the Aegisthus music in Scene 7). When the finale takes up the music of Elektra's monologue, the effect is simply of a final, clinching recapitulatory gesture – on the lines of Salome's concluding monologue – rather than of 'the last piece of the jigsaw falling into place'. The Triumph of Symmetry, as a dramatic device worked out to the last detail, is something more properly associated with Berg (*Lulu*!) than with Strauss.

The idea of a continuous musical *crescendo*, however, is Straussian through and through. Strauss himself described it in the following terms: 'After the recognition scene, which could only be completely realised in music, the release in dance' – drawing a parallel with the Dance of the Seven Veils in *Salome* ('the heart of the plot') and the 'dreadful apotheosis' of Salome's end.[21] The progression here is best described in terms of the relation between words and music, or, more specifically, between voice and orchestra. At the end of the opera Elektra dances herself to death. In this 'dance apotheosis', as Schnitzler calls it,[22] words are left behind as the orchestra swings into a waltz – one of the longest and most powerful of all Strauss's waltzes.[23] Elektra launches it with the words: 'Ob ich die Musik nicht höre? Sie kommt doch aus mir' ('You ask if I hear the music? It comes from me').[24] 'Musik' here means orchestral music, the triumph of the orchestra after nearly two hours of vocal domination. The whole opera, with its movement from oppression to liberation, is planned with this in mind. At the beginning (apart from the initial statement of the Agamemnon motive) the orchestra is kept in the background; its role is essentially that of commenting, through pictorial representation, on what the singers say. The vocal writing is a busy parlando, blossoming into lyricism for Chrysothemis and the recognition scene. The most lyrical vocal writing, however, is reserved for the finale, when vengeance has been done;[25] but at this very moment Strauss chooses to give the orchestra its head. It is as if words cannot express the joy of his characters; 'music' must do so instead.[26] (I shall return to this point at the end of the chapter.)

Ultimately, of course, any effect of rising tension is dependent on the drama. Without the dramatic situations – and the dramatic technique – that give rise to such tension, Strauss's scheme would go for nothing.[27] What we are dealing with is really a new kind of form, one in which both symmetry (that is, closed structure, the type of approach in which one half of a work can be superimposed on the other) and a continuous *crescendo* (an open-ended device) have their place. Such ideas are not incompatible, as superficially they might seem to be, because in music drama closed and open structures can coexist: indeed it is from their coexistence, from the alternation and overlapping of the complete and the incomplete, that the work derives its sense of 'unpredictable inevitability'.[28] Stravinsky criticised Wagnerian music drama for its 'improvisatory' quality, that is, for its formlessness; later Berg, in *his* music dramas, would bring back 'form' with a vengeance. *Elektra* stands halfway between these two extremes.

III

Closed structures in *Elektra* are defined first and foremost by tonality: thus the scene of the maids is 'in' D minor, Chrysothemis' speech 'in' E flat, Elektra's 'Von jetzt an will ich deine Schwester sein' ('From now on I will be your sister') 'in' G, her recognition aria 'in' A flat, her dance 'in' E. All of these passages (ranging in length from a page or two of vocal score to an entire scene) involve a strong V–I cadence;[29] and sometimes, as at the end of 'Von jetzt an' (just before Fig. 88a), the resolution is so decisive, and Strauss's difficulty in starting up again so apparent, that the music almost grinds to a halt. At such moments the work comes close to number opera. Robert Craft writes perceptively:

We have been conditioned to regard the 'progressive' aspects of many composers as the most important ones, and *Salome* makes that thesis difficult to disprove. (Whether the same can be said of *Elektra*, with its formal introductions to 'set' arias, depends on the listener's perspective vis-à-vis *Der Rosenkavalier* and *Ariadne*.)[30]

He also writes of *Elektra*'s 'almost mathematical form'.[31] Certainly the work is a far cry from Schoenbergian Expressionism, with its conscious abandonment of traditional formal categories. *Elektra* makes us realise the essential continuity of Strauss's œuvre: often described as a stylistic point of no return, after which the composer beat a quick retreat, it actually throws up as many points of contact with succeeding works as it does with preceding ones. Nevertheless the V–I cadences in *Elektra* are more disconcerting than those in *Der Rosenkavalier* and *Ariadne*, because the level of surrounding dissonance is higher.

This brings us to the matter of 'associative tonality', the principle of dramatic key association that Strauss inherited from Wagner.[32] It has become commonplace to say that E flat major, for example, is 'the key not only for Chrysothemis's first monologue, but also for the character throughout the opera'.[33] Similarly B minor is the key 'of' (or 'for') Klytämnestra, D minor 'of' Orestes, F major 'of' Aegisthus (Elektra is not associated with any particular key). This approach is taken to virtuoso extremes by Overhoff, who provides a page-long table of such associations.[34] But what does it mean to say that E flat, for example, is the key of Chrysothemis? Only that she has a big set piece in that key, which returns (as E flat minor) when *she* returns at Fig. 1a. However, this is partly a matter of thematic reprise: there is no sign of E flat when Chrysothemis returns yet again in the finale. As Arnold Whittall writes, with typical restraint:

The extent to which tonality functions associatively – thematically – may be debated . . . Such debates are incidental to the essential matter of acknowledging the existence of tonal structures which . . . underpin and promote the gradually-evolving coherence and continuity of the whole.[35]

Whittall devotes himself to such 'essential matter' in his chapter below.

Nevertheless the idea of 'associative tonality' is worth preserving, on historical as well as analytical grounds (and the tonal associations in *Elektra* are set out in detail by Tethys Carpenter below: see her Diagram 1). It was part of Strauss's 'simplistic' conception of the leitmotive – which must always be distinguished from his actual practice – that he associated certain motives with specific keys.[36] The Aegisthus motive in *Elektra* is a case in point. Whether or not 'essential', it is a matter of constant fascination how Strauss brings the music round to F major whenever the character is mentioned (see Figs. 39/4; 39/6; 69, together with the four preceding bars; 156; 213; 26a-32a *passim*, the interlude of the servants, who are creatures of Aegisthus; 39a/3; 47a). By the time Aegisthus finally appears (two bars before Fig. 199a), the association is so well established that Strauss merely writes a key signature of one flat; he does not introduce the actual motive until much later (Fig. 207a). More than that, he maintains the key signature throughout the entire scene, even though much of it (from Fig. 204a to Fig. 212a) comprises a closed structure in E flat.

The matter of key signatures is in fact of exceptional interest. (Key signatures in general are an unjustly neglected topic in musicology.) There are only twenty-three changes of key signature in *Elektra*, as compared with sixty-eight in the first act of *Parsifal* and 101 in the Prologue and first act of *Götterdämmerung* (to take two roughly comparable stretches from Wagner). This is a remarkably small figure, considering that *Elektra* is generally supposed to be a more 'advanced' work (and there are few passages where a key signature is abandoned entirely).[37] It suggests that although Strauss was occasionally more adventurous than Wagner at foreground level, his background thinking was more conservative.[38] But this is to raise the whole issue of whether Strauss was a conservative or a radical – a largely meaningless topic of debate since it assumes a historical norm. Arguments can be advanced for and against either side; they will never be resolved.[39]

It is more interesting to consider the stylistic discontinuities within *Elektra* itself, which can disconcert almost as much as the V–I cadences (which are of course one aspect of these discontinuities). The most disconcerting are probably those in the Klytämnestra scene, which progresses within the space of about thirty bars from eerie dissonance (Fig. 172) through echoes or anticipations of *Der Rosenkavalier* (173), *Das Rheingold* (three bars before 175) and Delius (*sic*, 175)[40] to eerie dissonance again (176) – and this is before she has even begun to describe her dream. But these can be justified on dramatic grounds. The '*Rosenkavalier*' passage, which might well sound queasy if taken out of context (but in a dramatic work nothing can be taken out of context), is actually a reminiscence of Elektra's 'honeyed'[41] phrases five bars after Fig. 148; it is *meant* to sound insincere. And the echoes of Wagner and Delius have their place in the chromatic intensification that follows. The foretaste of *Ariadne* in the recognition scene (Figs. 158a ff.) is interesting for a different reason: like the traces of number opera, it makes us realise the essential continuity of Strauss's œuvre.

Other 'echoes' can be explained (if not entirely explained away) in a similar fashion. For instance, the reminiscences of Brünnhilde that bother Craft[42] are explicable when we remember that Strauss conceived of his heroine as a 'goddess of vengeance'[43] (shades of *Götterdämmerung* Act II!). The 'Bavarian' music for Chrysothemis and the 'neo-classical' music for Aegisthus are all part of the general scheme.[44] Such discontinuities are less surprising when we consider that Strauss was a prolific song writer: the bulk of his songs (much earlier than *Elektra*, of course) startle with their stylistic contrasts, both within a set and within an individual number. We find similar contrasts in contemporary German song composers, notably Hugo Wolf, Hans Pfitzner and Othmar Schoeck.

IV

The domination of music at the end of the opera must be understood in the context of Schopenhauer's system of metaphysics. We have already seen Strauss writing that the recognition scene 'could only be completely realised in music'; in a letter to Hofmannsthal (22 June 1908), asking for more lines, he had said that he needed

a great moment of repose after Electra's first shout: 'Orest!'
I shall fit in a delicately vibrant orchestral interlude while Electra gazes upon Orestes, now safely restored to her. I can make her repeat the stammered words: 'Orest, Orest, Orest!' several times; of the remainder only the words: 'Es rührt sich niemand!' and 'O lass deine Augen mich sehen!' fit into this mood.[45]

In fact the words 'Es rührt sich niemand!' ('No one is stirring!') hardly make sense in the libretto as it stands. In the play they come in response to a line Strauss omitted, in which Orestes, after Elektra first cries out his name, warns her that, if anyone in the house has heard, 'that person holds my life in his hands'. Strauss evidently felt that the music would cover up the loss in verbal sense.

Elektra's final 'release in dance' takes the idea one stage further. As I have already suggested, Strauss's decision to give the orchestra its head at this point reflects a feeling that words cannot express the joy of his characters; 'music' must do so instead. This attitude finds its most famous expression in *The World as Will and Idea*:

Far from being a mere aid to poetry, music is certainly an independent art; in fact, it is the most powerful of all the arts, and therefore attains its ends entirely from its own resources . . . [In an opera libretto] the musical art at once shows its power and superior capacity, since it gives the most profound, ultimate, and secret information on the feeling expressed in the words, or the action presented in the opera. *It expresses their real and true nature, and makes us acquainted with the innermost soul of the events and occurrences, the mere cloak and body of which are presented on the stage* . . . The music of an opera, as presented in the score, has a wholly independent, separate, and as it were abstract existence by itself, to which the incidents and characters of the piece are foreign, and which follows its own unchangeable rules; it can therefore be completely effective even without the text. But as this music was composed with respect to the drama, it is, so to speak, the soul of this, since, in its connexion with the incidents, characters, and words, it becomes the expression of the inner significance of all those incidents . . .[46]

Strauss had read Schopenhauer in the 1880s and become one of the many artists (including Wagner, Schoenberg, Nietzsche, Proust and Thomas Mann) to be influenced by his work.[47] As a composer he must have been especially fascinated by what Schopenhauer wrote about music. For the philosopher, music is the highest of the arts because it is non-representational, that is, it articulates ultimate reality without going through the medium of ideas. One could say that Elektra dies because she can no longer live in a world of ideas; music has led her on to higher things.[48]

Of course all this had to work on the 'realistic' level, too. Hofmannsthal's stage directions describe Elektra as 'throwing back her head like a Maenad, thrusting her knees high in forward movement, flinging her arms wide apart'. As Kenneth Segar has noted, the reference is to the wild dance of the Bacchantes, followers of the god Dionysos,

performing their ecstatic celebration of the grandeur of life in all its destructive power. This is no longer Freud or Hermann Bahr, but Nietzsche's *Birth of Tragedy*: against the screams of the sacrificial victims (Klytämnestra, Aegisthus and their entourage) Elektra triumphantly asserts her fidelity to the dead Agamemnon as an expression of her oneness with the order of things. In dancing and dying, Elektra is both regaining the true self that she has had taken from her and is re-entering the ground of Being, a state in which she feels a heavy but visionary joy.

He adds that Hofmannsthal 'plays up every non-verbal means of creating mood and atmosphere', including décor, lighting, costume and gesture. The 'climax beyond words' was also an expression of his 'scepticism about the efficacy of language'.[49]

In view of Strauss's overwhelming orchestral conclusion (the only words after Elektra falls dead are Chrysothemis' unanswered cries to her brother), it seems a little mean of Heinz Politzer to say that 'the composer of the Dance of the Seven Veils does not achieve what the composer of *The Rite of Spring* could have'.[50] Elektra's dance takes its place in a long Romantic tradition of wordless operatic climaxes. The 'Liebestod', in which Isolde's voice is gradually lost in the sea of orchestral sound her words describe, is merely the most famous; the love scene from Berlioz's *Roméo et Juliette* (admittedly a choral symphony rather than an opera) another. The only one of Strauss's later operas to demonstrate the superiority of music over words in quite this fashion is *Daphne* (1937): here the spirit of Schopenhauer lives on in the oboe cantilena that takes over from the soprano as the heroine turns into a tree. Other orchestral, or nearly-orchestral, moments in the operas can be related to these: the *Rosenkavalier* trio might as well be wordless for all that one can hear the text; interludes in *Salome*, *Die Frau ohne Schatten* and *Intermezzo* (especially the lovely A flat one in the last, continuing the wife's thoughts after the curtain is down) convey ideas that the characters cannot, or dare not, express. But it is the 'moonlight' interlude in *Capriccio*, with the orchestra articulating the unspoken feelings of the Countess, that puts the matter in its proper, Straussian perspective. Strauss said the problem of 'words and music' could be solved only 'with a question mark'.[51] But he had forgotten his Schopenhauer: the philosopher could have told him – just as the orchestra tries to tell the Countess – that in opera it is music that has the last word.

4 Synopsis

The scene is the inner courtyard of the Royal Palace of Mycenae.[1]
The courtyard looks onto the back of the palace, which is dominated
by a huge pair of doors; on either side are low buildings in which the
servants live (male servants on the right, female on the left).[2] Night is
falling. As the curtain rises, five maidservants, supervised by a
woman Overseer, are drawing water from a well. Before any of them
speaks, however, the Agamemnon motive sounds *fortissimo* in the
orchestra. This tells us that the dead father, like the father of Hamlet,
is to be an important unseen presence throughout the work.[3]

But the maids have their minds on Elektra. It is, after all, the hour
when she laments her dead father. As if drawn by the mention of her
name, Elektra comes running out of the palace; but she springs
back, 'like a beast into its lair', when the maids turn towards her. 'Did
you see how she looked at us?' one of them remarks. 'Spitefully, like
a wild cat', says her companion. When two of them had approached
her the other day, a third chimes in, she had spat at them, comparing
them to horseflies: 'You should not suck sweetness from suffering.'
The Third Maid recalls her response: 'Yes, when you're hungry, you
eat, too.' This had angered Elektra so much that she sprang up,
extending her fingers like claws: 'I am breeding a vulture in my body.'
'That's why you're for ever crouching where the smell of carrion
attracts you', the Third Maid had replied, 'and scratching after
an old corpse!' At this Elektra had thrown herself into a corner,
howling.

The conversation presses on: 'Fancy the queen' – Klytämnestra, as
yet unnamed – 'allowing such a devil to hang about free in the
house!' Her own child, too. 'If she were my child', the First Maid
interjects, 'I'd keep her under lock and key!' By now the Fourth Maid
is beginning to feel some sympathy for the princess: 'Don't they treat
her harshly enough for you?' And the Fifth comes out with an unex-

pected tribute: 'I want to throw myself down before her and kiss her feet. Is she not a king's daughter? I want to anoint her feet and dry them with my hair.' At this the Overseer plainly feels that things have gone far enough. 'Get inside!' she barks. But the Fifth Maid is roused to an even more forthright defence: 'There is nothing in the world more regal than she is. She lies in rags on the doorstep, but there is nobody who can look her in the face!' The Overseer pushes her through the doorway on the left: 'Inside!' However, she can still be heard protesting: 'Not one of you is worthy to breathe the air she breathes!' Slamming the door (and possibly fearing a mutiny), the Overseer reminds the others of the abuse they have received from Elektra. She has even insulted their children: 'Nothing can be so accursed as the children that we have shamelessly conceived and borne in this house, where the stairway is slippery with blood.' Does she say this or not? 'Yes! Yes!' the maids fearfully agree, as they carry the water-pots into the house. 'Does she say this or not?' And as the door closes behind them, the voice of the Fifth Maid can be heard: 'They're beating me!'

For Theodor W. Adorno, Strauss was 'the master of the first 250 measures'; he regarded the maids' scene (which is actually nearer 200) as a 'high point which [Strauss] never again equaled'.[4] Whether or not we agree, it is impossible not to admire the composer's economy in getting important information across. Musical information as well as verbal: leitmotives are stated, each of the maids is individually characterised (the lyrical material associated with the Fourth and Fifth is perhaps the most memorable) and the whole scene has a gabbled, frenetic quality which is perfectly suited to the dramatic situation. Not that the words cannot be heard: indeed, the word-setting is one of the most remarkable aspects of the passage, prompting comparisons with composers as disparate as Wolf, Berg, Debussy, Mussorgsky and Janáček, as well as with the 'conversational style' developed by Strauss himself in later operas.[5]

II

The palace doors open again, and Elektra appears. 'Alone! Alas, all alone!' she begins;[6] 'Father is gone, shovelled away into his cold grave.' Putting her face to the ground, she calls his name. 'It is the hour in which they slew you – your wife and he who sleeps with her in one bed, in your royal bed.' She recalls the bath in which he was slain, and how Aegisthus dragged him headfirst out of the room while Klytämnestra finished the deed. 'Agamemnon! Father!' she cries.

'Don't leave me alone today! Show yourself to your child like a shadow in the angle of the wall!' Calling his name again, she promises that his day will come. 'As from the stars all time pours down, so will the blood from a hundred throats gush on to your grave!' Horses will be slaughtered in his honour; dogs, too; and 'We, we, your flesh and blood, your son Orestes and your daughters, we three, when all this has been performed . . . will dance around your grave.' Anyone who sees this dance will say: 'He is a happy man who has children to dance round his grave such royal dances of triumph! Agamemnon! Agamemnon!'

Musically the monologue is in three sections, articulated by the statements of Agamemnon's name. The first section (after the introductory, recitative-like 'Alone!') recalls his death: important motives associated with the royal family are introduced here. The second, shorter section presents the A flat melody sometimes linked by commentators with Elektra's childhood (it returns, again in A flat, during the recognition scene). The third and longest section recalls the murder music as Elektra promises that blood will flow, and then gradually turns into a waltz, the first of many anticipations of the waltz at the end of the opera. It is important to realise that Elektra does not actually dance at this moment;[7] she merely looks forward to her triumph.

III

A cry of 'Elektra!' breaks the spell. Chrysothemis, her younger sister, appears in the palace doorway. As if waking from a dream, Elektra forces herself to confront reality: 'What do you want? Why do you lift your hands like that?' But the dream still lingers: 'Thus did our father raise both his hands, but the axe fell and clove his flesh.' Chrysothemis tells her that 'they are planning a terrible thing', 'they' being Klytämnestra, their mother, who is now named for the first time, and Aegisthus ('that other woman', Elektra says scornfully). They are going to throw Elektra into a tower. Elektra's hysterical response – 'Open no doors in this house! The strangled breath, ugh! the death-rattle of murdered people', etc. – evokes an almost equally hysterical response from Chrysothemis. 'I cannot sit and stare into the darkness like you. In my breast there is a burning fire that sends me wandering round the house . . . I am so frightened that my knees shake day and night, my throat is choked, I cannot even weep . . . Were it not for you, they would let us go. Were it not for your hatred', she continues desperately, 'your unsleeping, uncontrollable spirit, they would let us out of this prison! I want to get out! Before I die, I want to live! I want to have children before my body shrivels up . . . Are you listening?'

Chrysothemis is now well into her 'big scene'. The recitative-like preparations of the early part of the dialogue have given way to an extended triple-time aria in Strauss's 'Bavarian' style, in short, another waltz. The 'middle section' describes Chrysothemis' loneliness: with father dead and brother away from home (he has been absent for many years), she sits with her sister like a couple of caged birds; and as she grows older she sees the women she knows having children, and the children themselves growing big.[8] This is the signal for the reprise, which ends with her pathetic cry: 'No, I am a woman and I want a woman's lot.'

Elektra reacts scornfully. 'Why are you crying? Get away! Go in! There is your place!' And they become aware of a noise within the palace. 'I can hear them running about. The whole household is up. Either they're giving birth or they're killing.' The orchestra is already preparing for the next scene: music reminiscent of the murder description replaces Chrysothemis' maunderings. Chrysothemis meanwhile remembers what she had presumably come to tell her sister, namely that Klytämnestra is in a bad mood. 'She has had a dream. I don't know what it was, I heard about it from the maids; they say she dreamed of Orestes, that she cried out in her sleep like one who is being murdered. They're coming now.' Torches and people, as yet dimly seen, fill the passage to the left of the door. 'Sister, when she is frightened, then is she most to be feared. Keep out of her way!' But Elektra is determined to talk to her mother. Chrysothemis flees.

IV

Now the orchestra comes into its own. 'A hurried procession rattles past the luridly lit windows: it is a pulling, a dragging of cattle, a muffled scolding, a quickly choked shouting, the hissing of a whip in the air, a struggle of fallen men and beasts, a staggering onwards.'[9] Strauss was never so happy as when writing to instructions such as these. The climax gradually becomes overwhelming. At last Klytämnestra herself appears in a window. 'Her sallow bloated face appears . . . still paler over her scarlet robe. She is leaning on her trusted Confidante, who is draped in dark violet, and on a begemmed ivory staff. A jaundiced figure, with black hair combed back, like an Egyptian woman, carries the train of her robe. The Queen is covered with gems and talismans; her fingers bristle with rings. The lids of her eyes are unnaturally large, and it seems to cost her an unspeakable effort to keep them from falling.'[10]

Elektra rises to her full height. Pointing her staff at her in rage, Klytämnestra calls on her attendants for support: 'Look there, all of you! See how she rears up with her neck swelling and hisses at me! And I let her live free in my house!' Then, lapsing into self-pity: 'Oh ye gods, why do you lay such a burden upon me? Why do you ravage me so? Why does this happen to me, eternal gods?' 'The gods?' repeats Elektra. 'But you yourself are a goddess!' Klytämnestra, confused, turns to her attendants again. They warn her that Elektra is being sarcastic. But Klytämnestra has been struck by something in her daughter's tone: it reminds her of sounds heard and forgotten long ago. Elektra, pressing home her advantage, reassures Klytämnestra (who is sentimental as well as exhausted) that she is no longer herself. 'That vermin is always hanging round you. What they hiss in your ears everlastingly tears your thoughts asunder, so that you go about in delirium, as though you were for ever in a dream.' Warming to these words, Klytämnestra decides to confide in her. She pushes her attendants aside ('What comes out of you is only the breath of Aegisthus') and demands to be left alone with Elektra.

All this is by way of preparation for what follows, an extended description of her dream. As her attendants retire and the torches disappear, Klytämnestra descends into the courtyard. Only a feeble ray of light from within the palace illuminates the figures of the two women. 'I have bad nights. Do you know of a remedy against dreams?' Elektra is evasive. 'As we grow older, we dream', Klytämnestra goes on. 'However, dreams can be dispelled.' That is why she wears so many talismans. But Elektra could help her: she is wise. Klytämnestra describes the terrible fears that overcome her at nights. When she sleeps, she dreams, she is immediately awake again – and 'not the tenth part of the water-clock has run out'. There must be an end to these dreams. Whoever is responsible for them, every demon will leave her alone as soon as the proper blood has flowed.

A sacrifice! Elektra's interest is at once engaged. The monologue becomes a catechism, with the mother asking questions, the daughter providing ambiguous answers. 'Which consecrated beast?' 'An unconsecrated one!' 'One that is lying bound, within?' 'No! It is running free.' 'And what sort of rites?' Wonderful rites, to be practised most strictly.' The waltz rhythm returns. 'Say the name of the sacrificial beast!' 'A woman.' 'One of my serving maids? A child? A virgin? A woman already known of men?' 'Yes! Known!' 'And how shall the sacrifice be performed?' 'In any place, at any hour of day or night.' 'But the rites! How should I put it to death? I myself must –' 'No. This time you do not go hunting with net and axe.' 'Who then? Who should kill it?' 'A man.' 'Aegisthus?' 'But I said a man!' 'Who? Answer me!'

Klytämnestra is tiring of the riddles. So, with a sudden change of tack,[11] Elektra asks her: 'Won't you let my brother come back home?' Naturally Klytämnestra does not wish to be reminded of the subject of her last bad dream. The very thought of it sets her trembling. Elektra takes comfort from this, knowing that it means Orestes is still alive. 'What does it matter to me?' Klytämnestra asks, regaining her composure. 'I live here and am the mistress. I have servants enough to guard the gates. And out of you I will get the right words one way or another. You have revealed that you know the proper victim . . . If you won't say it in freedom, you will say it in chains. If you won't say it fed, you will say it starving. I will find out whose blood must flow so that I can sleep again.'

Elektra leaps up enraged. 'Whose blood must flow? Blood from your own neck, when the hunter has caught you!' She paints a terrifying picture of Orestes searching the palace, rousing Klytämnestra from her sleep and pursuing her through the house (Elektra always at his side) until at last the axe falls. 'Then you will dream no more, then I need dream no more, and they who still live can exult and rejoice in their life!'

As they stand eye to eye, 'Elektra in wild intoxication, Klytämnestra gasping with horror', the Confidante comes running out of the palace and whispers in her mistress's ear. Klytämnestra's expression changes to one of evil triumph. This is the cue for another brilliant piece of orchestral tone-painting. She calls for lights; more lights; and rushes into the palace with her attendants. The orchestral climax is at its height. Then it is suddenly cut off as Elektra muses: 'What are they saying to her? She is pleased! What is the woman pleased about?'

V

The answer comes soon enough. Chrysothemis runs into the courtyard, whimpering like a wounded animal. Orestes is dead! Elektra cannot believe it. 'It is not true!' she keeps repeating. Chrysothemis fills in the story. 'The strangers were standing by the wall, the strangers who were sent to announce the news: two of them, an old man and a young one. Dead, Elektra, dead! He has died in a foreign land, killed by his own horses.' She sinks down beside Elektra on the doorstep.

The atmosphere is broken by the entry of a Young Servant, who comes hurrying out of the house, tripping over the sisters in the process. 'Out of my way! Hey there! You in the stables!' An Old Servant appears: what does this whippersnapper want? 'Saddle a mount, and as quick as you can! A horse, a mule, or, for all I care, a cow – but quick!' 'What for?' 'For him who orders you. How he stares! Quick, for me! For I have to go out to the fields to fetch the master.' He rides off to tell Aegisthus the news of Orestes' death. Hofmannsthal saw this scene as an interlude in the tradition of Shakespeare's comic servants.[12] It certainly breaks the tension; it also provides an extended anticipation of the music associated with Aegisthus, otherwise a rather shadowy figure.

Left alone again, the sisters consider the situation. Elektra has now digested the news she found so hard to accept, and indeed is already planning how to proceed. If Orestes is dead, the two of them – Elektra and Chrysothemis – must do the task together. 'What task?' Now it is Chrysothemis who appears slow to grasp what she is being told. 'Without delay it must be done. Be quiet. There is nothing to say. There is nothing to think about, save only: how we shall do it.' As the truth sinks in, Elektra reminds her that she has the axe. She was keeping it for Orestes; now they must wield it. 'A sleeper is a tethered victim. If they did not sleep together, I could do it alone. But as it is, you must help me.' Terrified, Chrysothemis can do little more than utter her sister's name.

The mood of scherzo has been maintained ever since the servants' 'interlude'. Now Elektra breaks it by launching into a waltz, this time in the 'Bavarian' style of her sister (it is all part of Strauss's large-scale scheme of recapitulation). She praises Chrysothemis' strength, her supple hips, her cool skin. 'With my sad, withered arms I embrace your body . . . I will sink my roots into you and infuse my will into your blood!' Trying to change the subject, Chrysothemis urges her to think of a way in which the two of them can get free. But Elektra persists: 'From now on I will be your sister as I have never been your sister before! I will sit by you in your room and await the bridegroom . . . You will shine through your veil like a torch as he leads you to the marriage-bed with his strong arms.' (The mood here is closer to *Der Rosenkavalier*: see Chapter 5, Ex. 6.) 'Oh yes! Far more than a sister am I to you from this day forth.' When Chrysothemis gives birth to a child, she, Elektra, will hold it on high. 'Your mouth is beautiful even when it opens in anger! Out of your pure, strong mouth a terrible cry must come, as terrible as the cry of the goddess of death, when they lie before you as now I do.' 'What are you saying?' 'That before you escape from this house and from me, you must do it! There is no way out for you but this.' 'Let me go!' is Chrysothemis' only response. Once again she flees.

VI

'Curse you! Well then, alone!' And Elektra begins to dig by the wall of the house for the axe. After a few moments she becomes aware of a stranger – Orestes, of course – watching her from the courtyard gate. She starts up violently. 'What do you want?' 'I must wait here.' 'Wait?' 'You must belong to the household? You are one of the maids from the palace?' 'Yes, I serve in the house.' The dialogue continues, slowly, like a litany; the underlying rhythm is that of a funeral march. 'I and another man have a message for the lady. We have been sent to her because we can bear witness that her son Orestes died before our eyes. I was his age, and his companion night and day.' 'Must I see you?' asks Elektra. 'Your mouth opens and shuts, and his is stopped with earth. You are alive and he, who was better than you, is dead.'

'Let Orestes be.' 'But what of me?' she wails (the music begins to move on here). 'To lie there and know that the boy will never come again, that those inside are alive and enjoying themselves, while I am here alone.' 'Who are you, then?' 'What does it matter to you who I am?' 'You must be of the same blood as the two who died, Agamemnon and Orestes.' 'Of the same blood? I am that blood! I am the shamefully outpoured blood of King Agamemnon!' And she identifies herself as Elektra. Orestes is at first staggered – he cannot get over her appearance – then overjoyed. 'Go into the house', she says; 'I have a sister there, who is saving herself up for festivities!' Unable to contain himself any longer, he tells her that Orestes is alive: 'He is as safe and sound as I am.' 'Then who are you?' The Old Servant comes quietly into the courtyard with three other servants. In a scene reminiscent of *Parsifal* Act III, they throw themselves before Orestes, kissing his feet and hands. 'Who *are* you, then? I am frightened.' He chides her gently: 'The dogs in the yard recognise me, yet my sister does not?'

Her cry of 'Orestes!' (to say nothing of the shattering orchestral chord)[13] ought to awaken the whole palace. But no one stirs. Instead the most lyrical music in the opera accompanies her growing recognition of him, the brother for whom she has waited for so long. She will not let him embrace him; self-conscious for the first time, she reflects on her ghastly appearance, her former beauty, the modesty she has had to sacrifice for the sake of their father. 'Do you think, when I rejoiced in my body, that his sighs and moans did not penetrate to my bedside? The dead are jealous.' Reminded of his duty, Orestes begins to tremble, and the most curious duet in all opera follows as Elektra takes pity, asking him if he will really perform the deed alone ('You poor child'). The waltz rhythms return, now merging with a kind of march: 'Happy is the one who comes to do the deed, happy the one who digs up the axe for him, happy the one who opens the door to him!'

They are interrupted by Orestes' Tutor, who appears in the courtyard gate. 'Are you out of your minds, not to restrain your speech when a breath, a sound, a mere nothing can destroy us and our work? She is waiting within. Her maids are looking for you. There is not a man in the house, Orestes!' A maidservant sets a torch on the doorpost. Klytämnestra's Confidante beckons to the two men to follow her into the house. The door closes behind them.

VII

Immediately Elektra realises that she has forgotten to give her brother the axe. There is a moment of suspense – in effect, another short orchestral interlude – while she waits. Then there is a piercing scream from Klytämnestra. Elektra cries out like a demon: 'Strike yet again!' A second scream. She stands with her back to the palace door as Chrysothemis and some maidservants run into the courtyard. General confusion. 'Something must have happened. She screams like that in her sleep. I heard men going in. Open the door for us, Elektra!' – and so on. Then the Fourth Maid cries out: 'Go back! Here's Aegisthus! Back to our rooms, quick! Aegisthus is coming through the courtyard.'

The ensemble (one of the few in the opera) quickly subsides. The maids run back to their quarters. To a motive which parodies that of Agamemnon, Aegisthus appears. 'Ho! Lights! Lights! Is nobody there to light me?' Elektra takes the torch from the doorpost and, running to Aegisthus, bows before him. 'What weird creature is this? What, you? Who told you to come to meet me?' And in a dialogue that is almost surreal in its impact, Elektra tells him that the strangers are waiting for him inside; that they have been received by a charming hostess; and that they are enjoying themselves in her company. 'What is there about your voice?' he asks suspiciously. 'Why are you staggering about like that with your torch?' 'All that has happened is that at last I have grown wise', she says. She moves around him in a weird dance (another waltz, of course). 'Why is there no light here?' he persists, in the doorway. 'Who are those men in there?' 'They are people who wish to attend on you in person, sir', she purrs; 'And I, who have so often intruded upon you boldly and presumptuously, will now at last learn to withdraw at the right moment.'

Aegisthus enters the palace. After a short silence, a noise breaks out. Aegisthus appears at a small window, shouting: 'Help! Murder! Help your master! Does no one hear me?' 'Agamemnon hears you!' Elektra retorts, as he is dragged away from the window to his death. Now Chrysothemis runs on again, this time with a crowd of women. 'Elektra! Come with us! It's our brother who is in the house! It is Orestes who has done it!' Voices from within repeat the name. Orestes' followers are fighting those of Aegisthus; bodies lie everywhere; a thousand torches have been lit. 'Orestes! Orestes!' 'Don't you hear it?' she demands. 'You ask if I hear it?' responds Elektra. 'If I hear the music? It comes from me.'

This is the beginning of the last waltz-sequence in the work. It extends until just before the end, sweeping everything before it as Elektra, more and more oblivious to what is going on around her, experiences the triumph she has so often imagined. 'The thousands who carry torches all wait for me: I know they are all waiting because I must lead the dance.' Suddenly she feels tired. Her duet with Chrysothemis continues, but her heart is not in it; she wants only to perform the dance for which she no longer has the energy. Chrysothemis eventually rushes into the palace to greet their brother.

And, summoning new strength, Elektra dances; it is a 'nameless dance', according to the libretto, though its origins in mythology are clear enough.[14] On and on it goes, an orgy of waltzing. After a while Chrysothemis appears in the doorway again, in front of an excited crowd. She calls to Elektra, but the latter tells her to be silent: 'For people as happy as we are, one thing only is meet: to be silent and dance!' She does a few more frenzied steps and then falls to the ground. Chrysothemis runs to her. Elektra lies rigid. The younger sister starts beating on the palace doors, now ominously closed (as Hofmannsthal hinted in a letter, Orestes is already being pursued by the Furies).[15] She cries out: 'Orestes! Orestes!' Silence.

5 *Dramatic structure and tonal organisation*

ARNOLD WHITTALL

I

Hugo von Hofmannsthal had little difficulty in demonstrating that *Elektra* was not, as Strauss had suggested in his letter of 11 March 1906, 'so similar to [*Salome*] in many respects'.[1] 'In *Salome*', the poet told the composer, 'much is so to speak purple and violet, the atmosphere is torrid; in *Elektra*, on the other hand, it is a mixture of night and light, or black and bright.' The dramatist saw the structure of his play as culminating in a 'rapid rising sequence of events relating to Orestes and his deed which leads up to victory and purification'. Whether or not victory and purification are opposites to be blended (like night and light, black and bright) or reinforced, their conjunction underlines those aspects of the play which convinced Hofmannsthal that his culmination could be 'much more powerful in music than in the written word'.[2]

All operas succeed to the extent that the music positively and memorably serves the drama. In *Elektra* there must therefore be a sense in which the music expresses hysteria, malevolence, menace, exultation. The light and bright side, represented most obviously by fraternal tenderness, is not excluded, but it is strictly subordinate. And this emphasis on the 'black' side has encouraged some commentators to attach the label 'Expressionist' to the work. *Elektra* is certainly different from *Salome*, principally because the relatively conventional confrontation between good and evil represented in the earlier opera is replaced by a study in pure fanaticism, Elektra's own strength confronting the weakness of Chrysothemis and Klytämnestra, and finding fulfilment when matched by Orestes' own implacable resolve. Someone encountering the music, and the story, for the first time might well expect that the sublime tenderness that descends on Elektra when she at last recognises her brother will effect such a profound change in her, and in the drama, that all

55

thought of revenge will dissolve, and she and Orestes will simply escape to a better life elsewhere. As it is, that brief tenderness merely serves to intensify Elektra's thirst for vengeance: it makes her cause not only just but practicable.

Since the drama itself is so obsessively concerned with dark moods and deeds, an ultra-Expressionist stream of consciousness might indeed have been an appropriate musical response. But Strauss, even in his most radical phase, was no Schoenberg. Nor was Hofmannsthal's text of the fragmented, allusive kind that Schoenberg set in *Erwartung* (1909), the archetypal Expressionist music drama. It is the force and density of Strauss's response that give *Elektra* Expressionistic attributes. Yet although the language has an extreme and sustained tension, it does not adopt the ultimate Expressionist resource, atonality. The musical organisation of *Elektra* serves to control the form as well as to enhance expression in relatively traditional ways, and, to this degree, the Apollonian undertow ensures that the Dionysian surface does not explode into a totally new kind of music drama. *Elektra* has motives, chords, cadences, textures, forms which, in principle if not in character, are comparable to those of compositions that deal with radically different subjects and express diametrically opposed moods. There is no mystery in music's capacity for deriving different kinds of expression from the same structural principles and formal procedures. But there is a very powerful tension in *Elektra* between formal control and expressive impulse.

Strauss's musical language at that time was fundamentally a dialogue between assertion and allusion, in the sense that two essentially opposed characteristics relating to tonality can be brought into a confrontation in which one (assertion) will triumph over the other (allusion). The pitch-language is therefore dichotomous, just as the rhythmic language is torn between fixity and flexibility. As often as the pitch-language alludes to tonality, extending or undermining it, it embraces, asserts it. Allusion and assertion interact and confront one another, as anticipation and act do in the drama. But in music where mediation between extremes risks diluting dramatic intensity, how can the composer sustain such a feverish pitch for so long? There must be contrasts which do not undermine momentum, and it will be argued below that Strauss is more successful with contrasts that intensify the allusiveness (the treatment of Klytämnestra) than with those that intensify the assertion (Chrysothemis). Even so, the justification for the ultimate triumph of assertion is its capacity to represent, at the end, the ultimate in hollow triumphs: the truly horrific 'fulfilment' with which the opera concludes, in a savage assault on memories of high-Romantic apotheoses, primarily Isolde's. A less elevated 'Liebestod' than Elektra's is difficult to imagine.

There is, however, another aspect to the question of structure in Strauss's opera, and this concerns form in the traditional sense. If Strauss initially resisted the idea of setting *Elektra* because of its closeness, as he saw it, to *Salome*, his decision to go ahead could have been the result of sensing that he could best do something *different* by building on the sure foundations of his existing achievements. And if Strauss's view of *Salome* as a 'symphony in the medium of drama' stemmed from the time of that work's creation, it might well have been the prospect of treating *Elektra* symphonically that won him over. (Strauss certainly spoke of his desire for 'symphonic unity' in 1909, when working on *Der Rosenkavalier*.)[3]

Commentators on *Elektra* have tended to accept this view, even to the extent of exploring analogies with the formal scheme of the sonata. As opera became more 'through-composed', it became relatively easy to detect elements of exposition, development and recapitulation – or, on a still larger scale, of first movement, slow movement, scherzo and finale. And since, as a composer of tone poems who had now turned to opera, Strauss was heir to both Liszt and Wagner, it seems apt to consider the relevance of Norman Del Mar's remarks about the form of *Salome* to its successor. In *Elektra*, no less than in *Salome*, Strauss might be held to develop the 'Lisztian organization and metamorphosis of motivic germs as in the symphonic poems. The result gives the opera a tremendous unity unusual in stage compositions outside Wagner's music dramas'.[4] And it seems equally reasonable for Del Mar to talk of Elektra's monologue ('Allein! Weh, ganz allein') as 'a finely constructed symphonic exposition' with the 'theme of the race of Agamemnon [the A flat theme beginning nine bars after Fig. 45] . . . the second subject, so to speak, of the symphonic scheme',[5] and also of the way Chrysothemis' themes are 'developed much in the manner of a huge symphonic second subject'.[6]

This point gains extra weight when tonalities are taken into account. Elektra's monologue is not exclusively in one key, but it could be argued that C (major and minor) is its most prominent tonal region: in which case, the E flat major of the Chrysothemis material suggests a conveniently close 'symphonic' relationship, befitting a 'second subject'. Needless to say it will scarcely do to assert that *Elektra* as a whole is 'in' C, in the way that Brahms's First or Bruckner's Eighth Symphony is in C. Even allowing for the late Romantic tendency for a tonality to fuse major and minor forms, and to combine with its major or minor relative into an extended tonic complex, the authority of a single tonic was not of limitless extent. It was nevertheless inevitable, in post-Wagnerian German music drama, that some degree of broad tonal planning would be part of the compositional process. (Even if Wagner did not, as Alfred Lorenz fantasised, construct the whole of *Tristan* around a mystically central E major, the tonal assertions and allusions of that seminal work, its recurrences and contrasts, are surely far from random or accidental.) It is not simply that in opera some themes and characters seem to belong to one key-area rather than another – alternatives would always be plausible – but that in the interests of balance as well as coherence, variety as well as unity, the harmonic flow should be controlled by the careful organisation of local and larger-scale relationships. What matters most, therefore, is not tonal planning in the abstract but the actual working-out of the dialogue between tonal assertion and allusion, affecting as it does all aspects of the musical material as it is shaped into a coherent design.

Strauss undoubtedly had basic harmonic considerations in mind from an early stage of *Elektra*'s evolution. Bryan Gilliam notes that 'harmonic annotations in the libretto form a fundamental part of Strauss's working method',[7] and he quotes a section of the text for the first Chrysothemis scene to which thematic, tonal, tempo and orchestral indications have been added by Strauss. In this case, Gilliam believes, the tonal 'basis' came first: Strauss began 'with a harmonic image that anticipates a short theme, which in turn provides essential material for a more extended, textless passage'.[8] Vocal lines may well be added at a relatively late stage, deriving from the orchestral melody. Nevertheless, it is important to emphasise here that much that is interesting and characteristic in Strauss's harmonic and tonal writing lies in the freedom with which he treats – even, perhaps, contradicts – this relatively strict, unified starting-point. In a work of such unrelieved intensity as *Elektra*, it was especially vital *not* to translate the obsession of the characters into a music whose contrasts were minimal. For this reason alone, it is surely the case that references to symphonic structure, or to a single, unifying harmonic process – significant though they may be – are ultimately of secondary importance. *Elektra* achieves a triumphant coherence through the subjugation of dangerous diversities: the text, and therefore the drama, demand no less.

II

Although not truly Expressionist, the musical language of *Elektra* is undoubtedly extravagant, and the dialogue between assertion and allusion functions at full power from the outset. The opening gesture of the opera – a portentously pure D minor fanfare, representing the slain Agamemnon – establishes a tonality that is by no means merely preliminary in the work as a whole. In the first scene, nevertheless, its hold is far less firm than such a straightforward opening might imply. Strauss retains the one-flat key signature throughout, but the tonality is extended and suspended more consistently than it is asserted. It is not simply abandoned, yet the emphasis on allusion stems from the allusions to Elektra herself. After her brief appearance early in this first scene, the hold of both diatonic D minor and consonant harmony remains tenuous, and Strauss uses the often savage nature of the references to Elektra in the remarks of the serving maids to sustain the dramatic image of a wild beast. Elektra is a cat who spits and wails, an animal nurturing another animal. The Fifth Maid has a different view, however, with an extravagant hymn to Elektra's supreme regality. At this point (Fig. 19) the arrival of a relatively unclouded D minor dominant seventh, anticipating the still stronger cadential preparation at the end of the Fifth Maid's interjection (Fig. 23), opens up the prospect of a more sustained, positive view of Elektra which is, of course, rejected (see Ex. 1).

Example 1

One important detail in the Fifth Maid's defence of Elektra is the appearance of the Agamemnon motive in the 'correct' B flat minor area, at Fig. 20. It is such anticipations of material used more fully later (as with Elektra's own theme) that help to integrate the opera's enormous, unbroken single span: in post-Wagnerian German opera a succession of scenes which have no themes (themes in a harmonic context, not just melodic lines or motives) in common is unthinkable; and changing perspectives on recurrent ideas are a particularly important structural element in a drama concerned with the inability to forgive or forget. Elektra's thirst for revenge is all-consuming, and the sheer solemnity with which she invokes her father determines the stark diatonicism of the music – six bars of sustained B flat minor harmony. (Adherents of the tonally unified view of the work will point out that just as the D of Scene 1 is the secondary dominant of the overall C, so this B flat is the secondary subdominant.) It is highly appropriate, given its formal role as 'exposition', that the music of Elektra's monologue should for the first time reveal the full structural potential of the work's language – unambiguous tonal assertion for its principal points of climax and emphasis, much less stable flux and allusion for the passages between, which need a particularly febrile momentum. A full account of this procedure would show how B flat minor is prepared, asserted, then (from Fig. 39) destabilised and ultimately replaced by a process that prepares the next point of assertion – C minor (Fig. 44). There is a sense in which, at the most basic level, the rest of the scene is concerned with repeating this process – that is, the (re-)establishment of B flat (now major), first at Fig. 53 and more conclusively at Fig. 56. There is then the progress through flux to the triumphant assertion of C (also major) at Fig. 61. But this second part provides a radical contrast in mood and style to the first, recalling Hofmannsthal's opposition of 'black and bright'. What transforms Elektra's mood appears to be her ability to imagine herself not simply as Agamemnon's child, but as *still* a child in his ghostly presence. It is the tender A flat music, to return in fuller form much later at her recognition of Orestes, which marks the pivotal point of change, between Figs. 45 and 46. It is not that, after this, Elektra becomes more gentle and conciliatory: on the contrary, she is simply more confident, more exuberant in her blood-thirstiness. The literal highpoints of this second stage of the monologue are the B flat on the word 'Grab' ('grave', three bars after Fig. 56) and the C on '*kö*nigliche' ('royal') at Fig. 61 (see Ex. 2). The dance of victory is also a dance of death, and the ground covered by

Example 2

the music in this scene is, in essence, that covered by the whole work. It is therefore much more than exposition in the symphonic sense. And it is also, as it must be if the opera is to be taken seriously, much more than the clinical close-up of a deranged harridan. Elektra's initial black mood is noble in its starkness, the pure, consonant diatonicism underlining the fact that she has been grievously wronged. In addition, her ultimate brightness has the heroic aura it needs if it is not to seem merely vulgar. After all, Elektra's principal quality is not that she is 'good' but that she is completely free of guilt.

The brightness becomes still more intense with the sudden shift at Fig. 63 from C major to E major, but this Agamemnon-centred assertion vanishes as Elektra is roused from her dream of vengeance by Chrysothemis. After monologue, dialogue, revealing that the difference between the two sisters, though extreme, is not total. Chrysothemis may be relatively naive and 'womanly', but her intuition is the more alert, as when she shrewdly states that 'were it not for your hate, your unsleeping, uncontrollable spirit, which they fear, then they would release us from this prison'.[9] The confrontations between the two inevitably make Elektra seem the more confident, not just the more cruel. But Chrysothemis could perhaps have seemed more sympathetic had Strauss made her music in this scene less of a glowing fertility dance. It is difficult to hear it now without sensing the *Rosenkavalier* waltzes waiting in the wings. And while Hofmannsthal must share the blame to some extent, Strauss's E flat major music conveys too little of her sheer desperation. It has ample rhythmic energy, but insufficient harmonic flexibility, as if it is meant to depict the joys of motherhood as Chrysothemis imagines them, rather than her actual frustration at being denied them. Yet if Strauss had intended to make this scene into the scherzo of an *Elektra* Symphony, he might well have provided just this kind of music.

It might be argued in Strauss's defence that only an extended display of artless exuberance from Chrysothemis could provide a sufficiently substantial contrast to what comes before and after. It is in any case vital to the drama that Elektra should be able, later on, to play on her sister's intense desire to procreate. There is also the point that Chrysothemis' own attempt to preserve a positive outlook in this scene does break down at the end when she reveals that she would rather die (the Agamemnon fanfare returns in the orchestra, three bars after Fig. 111) than endure this living death. In the end, freedom matters more to her than motherhood, and the chromatics that her music has managed to keep under control up to this point break out unrestrained. The Chrysothemis who announces Klytämnestra's approach has music essentially indistinguishable from her sister's. From Fig. 114 onwards the harmony is notable for disorienting the previously prominent E flat, and Strauss is not above using the time-honoured technique of sequence as generator of tension (from Fig. 118). As late as two bars before Fig. 129 elements of the E flat tonality are still apparent, but then these and other allusions are swept away in the turmoil as Klytämnestra finally enters (see Ex. 3).

Example 3

The scene between Klytämnestra and Elektra is discussed in detail elsewhere in this volume.[10] My own purpose is to emphasise its significance in the context of the work as a whole. It is the opera's central scene, and also, in places, its most extreme in style. Elektra herself may be half-crazed, but she feels no guilt. Klytämnestra is grotesque in her guilt, confronting the failure of all her attempts to ward off her premonitions of impending disaster. Her text hinges on pungent images of barrenness and corruption, explicit evocations of being devoured, of melting, which seem ripe for representation in a modern horror film. Even so, the part of the scene dominated by Klytämnestra is preliminary to its culmination, a second prolonged and anguished outburst from Elektra herself. In this, images of destruction pile on one another and embrace what must be one of the most palpable Expressionist states, the extreme agony of a soul that provides its own torment. As Elektra tells the cringing Klytämnestra: 'You are imprisoned within yourself as though in the red-hot belly of a bronze animal . . . Your soul is hanged in the noose you yourself have tied.' In its sheer relentlessness, this is one of the most harrowing episodes in twentieth-century music. Indeed, it may well seem self-defeatingly distasteful unless one can accept it as a necessary part of a drama that, for all its horror, does in the end offer the observer a genuine catharsis.

3: Richard Strauss with two of his first interpreters: Ernestine Schumann-Heinck (Klytämnestra, left) and Annie Krull (Elektra),

In the first part of the scene Strauss depicts Klytämnestra's agitation with some restraint. There is much quiet music here – a greatly needed contrast. Consonant triads are not infrequent and, depending on their context, may acquire local associations as tonics or dominants. The most extensive example of this – allusion becoming assertion before the focus is lost – is at Fig. 145, where Klytämnestra, sinking into a stupor, reaches into her memory for an image of security, associated with Elektra herself. Here the long F sharp major dominant, with plentiful $^6_4$s, supports the theme of filial tenderness, but it is nudged by Elektra's own more menacing motive onto an F sharp minor resolution (see Ex. 4). As the scene proceeds,

Example 4

Strauss makes telling use of ironic tonal symbolism as Klytämnestra's plea for 'respite from pain' moves from an E major assertion to C major (more dominant, no tonic) in a kind of sublimated allusion to Elektra's dance music.

As the memories of nightmare return the music advances into its most radical phase. Chords which could be used to clarify tonalities are still present, as they always are in Strauss, but they are either fleeting or overlaid with contradictory elements, until, at Fig. 200, as if to indicate Elektra's increasing control over events, a turbulent C minor is strongly asserted. With this, and the equally emphatic but transient B flat (major/minor) at Fig. 204, with its usual motive-complex, the elements are assembled for the rest of the scene. Klytämnestra herself slides further into ambiguous, unstable harmonic regions. By comparison, Elektra's assertions become almost blatant. At four bars before Fig. 230, C minor launches her long vituperative assault on her mother, and the essence of the musical structure here is once more the polarity of C and B flat, the bright and the black. By now, however, and with startling impact, the two moods and shades have become fused. Between Figs. 258 and 259 the triumphant C major dominant, complete with Elektra's high C, is diverted (with a wrenching chromatic progression that will return to influence the final bars of the work) to resolve onto the tonic of B flat major, with the word 'freun' ('rejoice'). There could hardly be a more arresting image of the supreme confidence inseparable from intense instability (see Ex. 5).

In what Strauss by his Figure-numbering (1a etc.) encourages us to regard as the second half of the opera, the sense that elements already stated are being developed and simultaneously recapitulated fits well with the unfolding of the drama; obsessions and desires expressed in the first half are ultimately fulfilled or conclusively frustrated in the second. Only some of the ways in which the second half might be felt to allude to the first can be conveyed here, and in any case it is vital to the momentum of the drama that we should not have the feeling of beginning again after Klytämnestra's exit. Rather we move inexorably onwards, with increasing intensity, dragging with us memories of the past – sometimes literal, sometimes distorted. Thus the D minor focus evident in the early stages of the second scene between Elektra and Chrysothemis might seem a deliberate reassertion of the tonal and harmonic character of the very first scene of the opera.[11] Yet the main motivic element here is not the Agamemnon fanfare but the idea associated with Elektra's

Example 5

tender memories of happy childhood – now impassioned rather
than tender, as it accompanies her refusal to accept her sister's claim
that Orestes is dead. The section between Figs. 4a and 25a is one of
Strauss's finest pieces of operatic-symphonic composition in the way
a finely controlled and directed thematic-harmonic process, skilfully
integrated despite the many shifts of tonal perspective, creates
appropriate space for the eloquent declamation of the vocal lines.
The scherzo for the servants is very brief, without time for it to seem
too incongruous an attempt at light relief. Then, from Fig. 34a,
comes the scene in which Elektra attempts to seduce her sister into
complicity in murder by explicit promises of erotic fulfilment. The

principal tonal and metrical association here (from Fig. 52a) is, appropriately, that of Chrysothemis' own earlier, E flat major, out-pouring, but with an even stronger tendency to slip sideways into remote regions: thus the progress from the E flat tonic of Fig. 52a to its dominant at Fig. 56a is anything but straightforward, the deviousness in the music as blatant as in Elektra's honey-venomed words. As a whole, however, the music from Fig. 52a to Fig. 68a firmly reinforces the E flat major tonality, and the presence of such a passage is vital to the coherence of the drama, harnessing as it does the more wayward energies of the long episodes where focus is less clear, harmony less stable. After the emphatic cadence at Fig. 68a the E flat focus begins to dissolve, and it is almost as if, in maintaining its metrical and motivic character while allowing the fundamental language of the music to veer towards atonality, Strauss is producing a parody of the heroic style he himself knew so well. When a clear tonal focus is restored – G major (at Fig. 82a), with a quite different mood and metre from what precedes it – Elektra's more tenderly seductive music seems to prefigure the gentle pages of *Der Rosenka-valier* (see Ex. 6). Then, with maximum musico-dramatic cunning, Strauss uses Elektra's promise to attend her sister like a slave to bring back music associated with the Fourth and Fifth Maids in Scene 1 (Fig. 89a). Once again, therefore, a D tonality is touched on, and reinforced with the switch to D major at Fig. 92a.

If Strauss had the reputation of being a cerebral composer, one might choose to argue the case for whole-tone structuring on the highest level in *Elektra*:[12] E, D, C, B flat and A flat are all especially important harmonic centres, and at the climax of this second Elektra/Chrysothemis scene the music drives itself through an ex-traordinary confrontation between dark B flat minor (before Fig. 98a) and desperate D major to one of those particularly decisive and literal full closes in C minor (Fig. 102a). This one is much more an end than a beginning, however, for what follows, up to the point where Orestes speaks for the first time (Fig. 123a), is too fast and furious to remain firmly focused harmonically for any length of time. When the turmoil does subside, it is, once again, D minor that achieves the greatest stability, and its cadential reinforcement at the words 'Herold des Unglücks!' ('Misfortune's herald!', Fig. 128a) well summarises the moods of foreboding and despair that particularly belong to that key in the opera. After a further D minor full close at Fig. 130a the music begins to weave away from such clarity, not decisively, but in answer to the increasing emotion in the exchanges

Example 6

between brother and sister as the moment of recognition approaches. Steadily building an effective, highly dissonant – even, in local terms, atonal – climax (Fig. 144a) is one thing. But it would have been fatally easy to make the reverse process, gradually winding down from this high point to a moment of quiet and diatonic calm, a decline into sheer sentimentality. Strauss avoids this partly through his instinct for pacing. He refuses to be hurried, and yet the means whereby dissonances resolve, and a kind of fiercely distorted B flat dominant finally becomes a pure A flat dominant, are so finely controlled that there is never a jolt, even at the dangerous moment where the bass ceases to move by step and falls from G to E flat (six bars after Fig. 147a: see Ex. 7).

Example 7

Having achieved this remarkably convincing transition, Strauss is careful not to linger for too long in what is, essentially, an unreal atmosphere. Elektra cannot let herself be distracted more than momentarily from her mission, and so the haven of A flat major is soon lost for ever. At Fig. 157a there is an assertion of C minor, with the Agamemnon fanfare, as an earnest of the truly central concerns of the drama. And what is particularly notable, and new, is that, with Orestes present, Elektra's music mixes bright and dark allusions much more evenly – as in the way the sharp-side material from Fig. 163a balances flat-side material, for example. As the drama moves towards its apex, the central musical concerns are also reiterated, notably, after Fig. 172a, the progression from a C (major) dominant to a B flat (minor) tonic. But Strauss does not allow himself to be tied down too soon. The C major focus of the scene's rhetorical climax (Fig. 177a) is therefore diverted to E and, finally, back to D minor, three bars before Fig. 181a.

In the melodramatic scene of Aegisthus' baiting and murder which follows, it could well be argued that atmosphere is all and that the actual pitches scarcely matter: others could create a suitably sinister texture just as well. But Strauss did nevertheless make certain decisions that seem of more than purely local significance, like using chords of C major and minor as if they were reminders of the drama's principal purpose, and exploiting his habitual 'waltz metre/ E flat tonality' pairing for the grotesque music in which Elektra mockingly urges Aegisthus on his way to death. Otherwise Strauss, the good music-dramatist with his eyes firmly on symphonic analogies, uses this scene as a means of developing the material associated with the male servants that briefly interrupted the second Elektra/Chrysothemis scene. The work's more essential motivic elements retreat in order to make their reappearance in the opera's final stages the more arresting. And these final stages can be said to begin with Elektra's great cry: 'Agamemnon hört dich!' ('Agamemnon hears you!', Fig. 216a), to a C minor chord which, for the moment, establishes no larger-scale tonal connections, yet still initiates a process that will only be completed in the work's last bar.

These final stages crucially confirm the validity of identifying close associations between dramatic events and musical presentation (especially harmony, the most fundamental element of that presentation) as the essence of Strauss's musico-dramatic technique in all its mastery. The closing scene is more a matter of strong and changing moods than of a sequence of events. It can be summarised as follows. Chrysothemis ecstatically recounts the brutal triumph of Orestes: 'All that are living are spattered with blood.' Elektra's response is a different kind of ecstasy, and there are further analogies with Wagner's Isolde in her moment of ultimate rapture, deaf to

anything and anyone outside herself. The long-anticipated fulfilment of her lust for vengeance does not free Elektra from this terrible solipsism. She can only transform herself into an embodiment of
victory by dancing and dying. Having accomplished her earthly task,
she is already with the gods. Her ultimate moment of truth confirms
to her that 'love kills' – she has after all been kept alive only by hate
– and it is this love that ensures her a place with the immortals. And
although, after this, Elektra does appear to become aware of her surroundings and to issue orders, she acts only to hasten her own
oblivion.

In the music Strauss has no difficulty in giving all the essential
motives a final form consistent with the mood of triumph, and with
the insistent rhythms of Elektra's dance. In the first stages a purely
tonal brightness (E major), which has been touched on before but
kept in reserve, now bursts forth with jubilant incandescence. It
alternates (Fig. 226a, then 236a) with C major – less bright, but more
a central structural force in terms of the work as a whole – and
although both keys are subject to extension, sometimes involving the
clear assertion of other regions, there can be no denying their joint
supremacy. But the truly musical denouement of the drama is determined by Strauss's decision to depict death as *dark*, which means
that the bright tonalities must disintegrate and finally be replaced.
Between Figs. 258a and 259a a progression by chromatic steps in
the bass to restore the C major dominant 'overshoots' by one step,
thereby attaining the extreme brightness of a B major dominant. But
instead of preparing the restoration of E major, this drives the music
into a frantic flux (Elektra 'makes a few more steps of uncontrolled
triumph') from which emerge the final alternations of E flat minor
(Elektra lifeless) and C minor (Agamemnon avenged) (see Chapter
6, Ex. 14). Because of the common pitch E flat the two chords are not
in unresolved opposition, of course. Rather, they form a unified
tonal complex of which C is the central element. Nevertheless,
Strauss decides to extend the complex by one final factor. There may
be no way of knowing whether he might have first written C *minor*
chords in the last four bars. But in deciding to make them major he
underlines that Elektra's victory is not diminished but fulfilled by her
death. It might almost be a peculiarly Expressionist kind of happy
ending, were it not for the brutal juxtaposition of the very last bar.
Does the 'gesture' matter more than the fact that these chords are
E flat minor and C major? By no means: Strauss has chosen a pro-
foundly convincing way of ending the opera with specifically dark

and bright elements in equally brutal guise. He thereby sets the seal on one of the most sustained demonstrations to date of music's ability to represent extreme emotions through an extravagantly rich yet formidably coherent structure.

6 The musical language of 'Elektra'

TETHYS CARPENTER

I

When Schoenberg in a letter of 1914 wrote to decline an invitation to say something in honour of Strauss's fiftieth birthday, his condemnation of the older composer seems to have been almost complete: 'He is no longer of the slightest artistic interest to me, and whatever I may once have learnt from him, I am thankful to say I misunderstood.'[1] Schoenberg's principal objection to Strauss – apart from his professional grudge – was moral; it is clear he felt him musically to be beneath contempt. By this date his opinion would have been coloured by *Der Rosenkavalier*, but it is interesting to speculate on what he might have felt five years earlier about *Elektra*, for although its music is indeed morally suspect – and invariably misunderstood – it is also clever, far cleverer than *Salome* (which Schoenberg is known to have admired), and implies that Strauss knew a good deal more about the supposedly abstract principles of ordered atonality than the incipient dodecaphonist might later have cared to acknowledge.

The musical language of *Elektra* certainly sounds advanced. It is generally considered to be Strauss's most modern work, an Expressionist extravaganza from the destructive consequences of which he was gradually to retreat. As in *Salome* the music provides a brilliant and graphic illustration of the libretto, whose greater horrors can be seen to have 'objectified and validated Strauss's emancipated dissonances'.[2] The sheer strangeness of Klytämnestra's dream, with its 'psychological polyphony',[3] has prompted comparisons with *Erwartung*; full dramatic use is made throughout of leitmotives, pictorial or characterising tonalities and sonorities, bold harmonic effects (including piled-up dissonance, whole-tone or tritonal chords, bitonality, unexpected modulation – or loss of apparent key altogether) and, most of all, the orchestra, which both reflects the smallest subtlety on the surface of the action and gives the opera its backcloth of relentless harshness. Musical exaggeration and diversity would seem to be justified by the violent and opposing demands of the drama.

Such a view need not suggest formlessness: *Elektra* is often regarded either as a large-scale dramatic symphony or symphonic poem (complete with first and second subjects, properly, if freely, developed and recapitulated)[4] or simply as architectural form 'with its construction based on massive pillars of sound',[5] the pillars or climaxes being dependent on the formal subsections in the text. Strauss himself admitted to being unable to compose without a programme: thus, Expressionist freedom within an external imposed (or chosen) frame.

This is a description one might with some accuracy apply to *Salome*, which is almost too full of different ideas, all played off against each other in a sort of exotic collage but not inherently unified. Formally, the libretto has dictated its own precise outline, which is matched with a strong and symbolic key structure; the music is tonal, and resolves tonally. But much of the music in between, however beautiful or effective, remains disjunct (as it had, to a far greater extent, in the more overblown tone poems). There is still, despite the Wildean clarity and Strauss's own musical 'solution', a lack of compositional constraint or control of some material: it is – not inappropriately, as it happens, to the story – too diverse to be disciplined.

But *Elektra* does not give this impression: it is aurally more 'difficult', less lyrical and less tonal, yet sounds tauter and more coherent. The obvious explanation for this – Strauss not being a composer one naturally associates with self-discipline for its own sake – has been, first, that Hofmannsthal's play is more tightly organised than Wilde's (which is exact and lucid but with an ornate and rhapsodic *fin-de-siècle* overlay), built in discrete blocks which are starker and though not more strictly segmented more transparently so, and, second, that the heroine is motivated not by a perverted eroticism awakened halfway through the opera but by a fanatical and unswerving desire for revenge: Elektra has nothing if not a sense of purpose. As before, Strauss echoes both form and purpose in his tonal plan (see Diagram 1, Ex. 1), which, centring on Elektra's progress from despair to triumph, presents each character and state of mind in its own particular key or mode.[6] But although these keys are manipulated with great skill, providing a detailed and recognisable account of the action and giving an underlying firmness to individual

Diagram 1

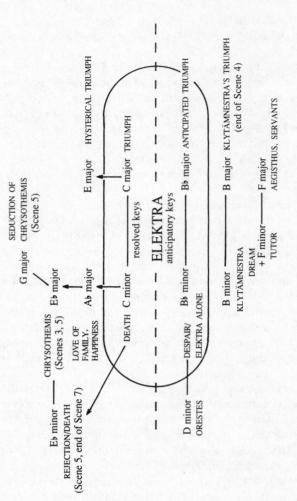

Example 1

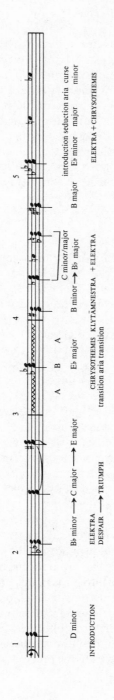

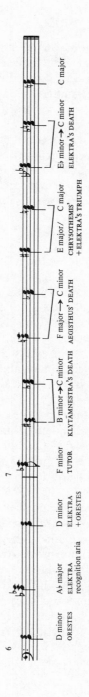

sections, they merely add to the frame and do not actually propel it, for here the focus of the *musical* action is no longer tonality *per se* (articulated as a tonal opposition in *Salome*) as dynamic expression of dramatic intent, but tonal – or, more specifically, bitonal – procedure. It is almost as if Strauss, full of confidence after his recent *succès de scandale*, decided that conventional structure could be taken for granted rather than battled with, and that he would instead concentrate on controlling just those sections which had previously appeared to offer the perfect opportunity for unbridled excursions into the realm of sensational effect or sonority: effect is now his structural starting point.

II

In *Salome* the most shocking sort of harmonic effect Strauss had been able to come up with had been the deliberate and unprepared superimposition of unrelated triads. There he uses them either pictorially, to convey an emotion, as in Salome's furious chord of contradiction (Fig. 98: E flat major/F sharp major in root position, though well muddled, or [0,1,4,6,9], 5–32),[7] or to depict conflict of will, such as the Jews' polyphonic dispute – to which his much-quoted remark about 'horizontal' hearing[8] refers – or Jochanaan's and Salome's hostile but motivically linked E flat minor/A major ([0,1,4,6,7,9], 6-Z50). In *Elektra*, he has taken exactly the same sort of superimpositions, but here they signify not external conflict but the complicated and disturbed state of a single character: they are internal to the drama from the outset.

Elektra herself is portrayed by the chord first heard at Fig. 1/6, which appears to be D flat major over E major, both in root position, or 5–32 ([0,1,4,6,9]), and which is usually, though not invariably, presented and spelt in this form, often at pitch.[9] It has a very specific sonority which tends to sound more or less distinct from its surroundings, but it is integrated into more 'normal' contexts in a number of ingenious ways. At Fig. 1/6 the blow is softened by the retention of the pitch classes 5 and 8 (F and A flat) from the preceding *fortissimo* F minor $^6_3$ chord, and it dissolves into an E major $^4_2$ (see Ex. 2). Elsewhere Strauss seems to have no particular trouble getting onto the chord, mainly because it is so often inserted as a savage interruption to highlight a reference to Elektra's bitterness and anything too straightforward would be beside the point: if there is a connection, he tends either to hold notes over from the previous chord (Ex. 3a) or

Example 2

[5,4,1,11,8]   E major $\frac{4}{2}$
[0,1,4,6,9] I$_5$
5–32

to approach it via semitone, often, but not necessarily, in the bass (Ex. 3b). Getting off it again may provoke a similar response (Exx. 4a and b); he may alter the chord so that it acts as a functional harmony (Ex. 4c) or simply treat the chord itself as one (Exx. 4d and e).[10]

Example 3

C♯ minor [0,1,4,6,9] I$_5$ [0,1,4,6,9] I$_5$

Example 4a

[0,1,4,6,9] ——— A♭ retained ——————→ G♯
                    D♭ major   E major $\frac{4}{2}$

See also Figs. 162/5, 82/7–9 (use of Elektra's *motive* to imply Aug. 6)

Example 4b

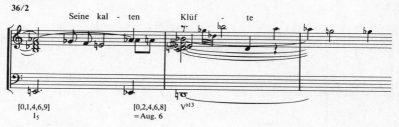

[0,1,4,6,9]　　　　　　[0,2,4,6,8]　　$V^{\flat 13}$
I_5　　　　　　　　　= Aug. 6

By semitone progression

Example 4c

→ $F\sharp^7$: Alteration by addition for incorporation into tonal sequence.

[0,1,4,6,9] I_9　　　　[0,1,3,4,6,9] $I_9 = A\flat^7$
　　　　　　　　　　　　　6-27

(Cf. *Salome*, Fig. 360/6)

Example 4d

Vocal part	$\flat 6$	$\hat{5}$	$\hat{1}$
implies	II	V^7	I
or Neapolitan	$\flat II^7_6$	V^7	I
(D♮ = E♭♭ or ♮$\hat{3}$)			
bass line suggests	♮III	V^7	I
	[0,1,4,6,9] I_3		

Example 4e

[0,1,4,6,9]　　　　　　　　　　　　[0,1,4,8]
I_5
upper line　$\hat{3}$　　　　　　　　　　$\hat{5}$
　　　　　(I　　　　　　　　　　　　V)
bass　$V^{6\,(\flat 13)}$　　　　　　　　　V^7
(Cf. Fig. 169)

THE OPERA THAT WILL "ELEKTRIFY" LONDON.

TO SING THE MOST ARDUOUS SCORE EVER WRITTEN: CHARACTERS IN STRAUSS'S "ELEKTRA," TO BE PRODUCED FOR THE FIRST TIME AT COVENT GARDEN ON SATURDAY.

ΕΛΕΚΤΡΑ

4: The first London performance of *Elektra* (first Beecham Opera Season at Covent Garden, 1910): Friedrich Weidemann (Orestes, inset left), Edyth Walker (Elektra, inset right), Anna Bahr-Mildenburg (Klytämnestra)

Sometimes 5–32 will appear in the middle of an extended sequence
in which it will have been most logically prepared as part of a tonal
progression, as at Fig. 98a/9, over a descending, and 180a, an ascending, bass line: it is instantly audible, but because of what now sound
like added inner voices. Klytämnestra's notorious description of her
night horrors at Fig. 186/7 (Ex. 5) works on the same principle,

Example 5

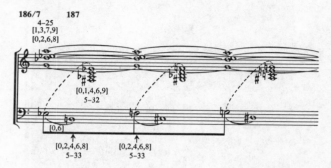

but here the tonal overlay to the rising bass has been replaced by a
static whole-tone pedal, giving a much more rigid alternation of
sonorities and, though the pattern is equally logical, altogether
losing the sense of tonal direction. On several occasions [0,1,4,6,9]
becomes the dominant sonority, setting up its own sequence (Figs.
232–3, where the infill is tonal, Figs. 114/8–118, where it is decorated
with parallel or contrary motion,[11] or Figs. 39–40, where there is no
infill). It may not be 'resolved' at all, whether in these circumstances
or in predominantly conventional ones (Fig. 39/7); or it might
simply be proclaimed in isolation as a colour chord (Fig. 189a – its
meaning is explicit).

Klytämnestra is also characterised by a bitonal combination,
B minor plus F minor, giving the set [0,1,3,6,7,9] or 6–30, presented
together at the start of her dream aria (Ex. 6). In this case the
F minor triad is manifestly superimposed: there is no note in common and, rather than treating the set as an indivisible unit like
[0,1,4,6,9], Strauss here plays on the incompatibility of the tritone
between its parts, setting one stridently above the other after a crot-
chet's rest and letting it slide down to a consonance. Because of this,
B minor, Klytämnestra's underlying 'associative' tonality, sounds
dominant, and he makes use of this imbalance to produce clashes

Example 6

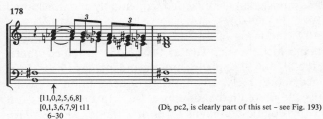

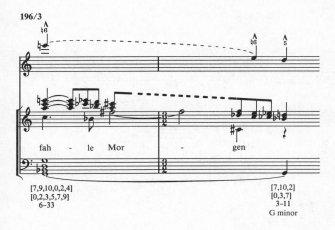

which are perhaps best described as complex appoggiaturas, such as the A minor against G minor at Fig. 196/3 (Ex. 7), rather than chords in their own right. Often the two triads are juxtaposed instead of superimposed; this is how the set is introduced in the first scene

Example 7

(Fig. 1/3) and how it frequently recurs as a violent representation of Elektra's hatred of her mother (at Fig. 190a, for instance, where she waits for Klytämnestra's death). It may be incorporated thus as a passing reference into an alien texture or even motive (Fig. 39a/7: at the words 'sprichst du von der Mutter?' it intrudes into the three-note *marcato* motive of Elektra's resolve – see Ex. 9a – in unusually subdued scoring). Nonetheless, it must be regarded as fundamentally a single unit; it does appear as such (Fig. 64/4), and like 5–32 –

though to a much more limited extent, for its allegiance to the B/F axis seems almost unshakable – it is used sequentially and transposed (Figs. 195–195/6, Fig. 29/6).

At Fig. 192/5, following one of the most disturbing passages of her narration, in which the three strata of Ex. 5 (the sustained whole-tone cluster, the [0,1,4,6,9] sequence and the independent bass) have been developed more freely, Klytämnestra's description of living decay prompts the more dissonant chord 7–31. In fact, this is still 6–30, now in the double-dominant form of C major and F sharp major, preparing for the return of B minor/F minor at Fig. 193, the next subsection, but over an E flat retained from 5–33 of the previous bar, which confuses matters, especially as Strauss then, instead of simply resolving the two Vs, fudges the issue by reinterpreting E flat as D sharp, or $\sharp\mathrm{III}^7_{\sharp 3}$ in B minor, with an altered version of one of Klytämnestra's motives (from Fig. 67/6), from which he pivots (Ex. 8). He is remarkably good at extricating himself from such

Example 8

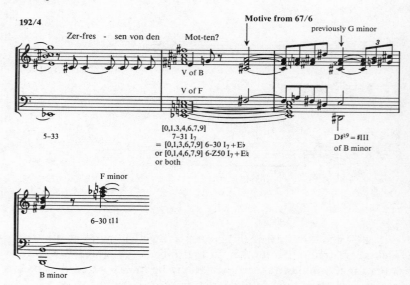

situations in the shortest possible time, either by pivoting[12] or by semitone; the suspended diminished seventh over Orestes' D at Fig. 214/7 becomes V^7 of A flat in this manner – a very bad moment, were it not important to link the two keys so conspicuously for other reasons. Indeed, most of his progressions from dissonances (including [0,1,4,6,9]) require that he ignore some notes in favour of others, which is usually his favourite method of modulation in any case ('Von jetzt an will ich deine Schwester sein', at Fig. 82a, has some especially slippery semitonal examples (see Chapter 5, Ex. 6)): it makes no difference if there are, briefly, a few 'wrong' notes in his voice leading. Thus, Fig. 192/5 itself could also be interpreted as 6-Z50, the most extreme bitonal opposition, used at Fig. 11a – 'Es ist nicht wahr!' – as E flat minor on A major, and equally suitable to the extremely unpleasant disintegration of which Klytämnestra speaks, with an extraneous E♮, later ♮9 of D sharp[7]. That this is actually contraindicated both by the context and by the use of 6-30 several times in the preceding bars (for instance, at Fig. 191/6) one might feel was not strictly relevant, given Strauss's remarkable facility in managing and manipulating his materials: one is always left slightly wary by his touches of opportunistic inconsistency. On the other hand, the suspension at Fig. 144a, parallelling Fig. 11a, which is more complex, perhaps vindicates other seemingly looser configurations: more on this later.

Of all the characters in the opera, only Elektra and Klytämnestra, the one compelled by fierce hate to a destructive triumph and the other consumed within herself by guilt and yet defiance, are projected bitonally. As we have seen, 5-32 and 6-30 can be adapted to suit a wide range of tonal situations or assume their own pseudo-tonal function. However, though they are as dualities vividly expressive of their various purposes their largely irrelative presence as such does not – and could not – actually account for the degree of cohesion felt *between* them and the surrounding non-bitonal textures. Some, at least, of the impression of increased compositional control is due to the constant tendency to sequence (already noted *en passant*), to the formulation of sometimes intractable material into regular and intelligible patterns, whether on a small (Figs. 26–27/7, Fig. 143a/9) or a more extended scale (Figs. 242a/4–244a, Figs. 256a/6–258a/5). Very often, such patterns will lead up to a cadence, and such cadences are frequently sharply articulated, both by an unusually strong dominant–tonic relationship and by the emphatic vocal accentuation of the ends of sections – or arias – at the climax of which the orchestral accompaniment may suddenly drop out, stressing by its absence the decisiveness of the closure (Figs. 61–2 (see Chapter 5, Ex. 2), Fig. 108a/13, Fig. 229a/9); the start and finish of all formal divisions are clearly marked. Not content merely with this, Strauss has also put together a useful collection of modulatory formulae which are neither specifically leitmotives[13] nor necessarily referential in any definite sense but which function as the cornerstones between sections or as punctuation marks within, conveniently bridging gaps between distant tonalities and demarcating structure (Ex. 9). Nevertheless, these factors cannot in themselves affect the internal musical continuity but only circumscribe it. Indeed, the coherent nature of that continuity cannot be seen to result from any such external device but rather derives from Strauss's far more sophisticated treatment of the inherent implications of bitonality itself.

Example 9a   Example 9b

Example 9c   Example 9d

Example 9e(i)

Example 9e(ii)   Example 9e(iii)

178/6

246/3

[0,4,8]
D major/B♭ major

C♯¹³   B♭⁷

('die Bräuche
sind noch
nicht erfüllt')

Example 9f

135

[0,4,8]   B

Example 9g(i)

258/3

jauchzt! und   kann sich sei - nes   Le - bens freun!

C major   F♯⁷   F⁷   B♭ major

See Figs. 112, 172a/6, 74

Example 9g(ii)

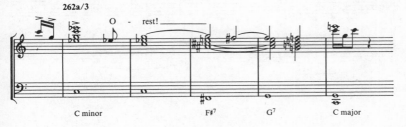

262a/3

O - rest!

C minor   F♯⁷   G⁷   C major

At Fig. 138/3, as Klytämnestra asks 'Warum bin ich lebendigen Leibes wie ein wüstes Gefild?' ('Why is my living body like waste ground?'),[14] Strauss introduces a new harmonic motive which is to persist in the same form throughout the central Scene 4 and return in answer as the signal for her death at Fig. 185a. Del Mar comments that 'this apparently new theme contains within its structure the opposition of two minor chords a tritone apart . . . This motivic harmony steadily gains in importance as the scene progresses.'[15] He is referring to the E–B flat in the upper part, but is more accurate than he knows, for here is set down the progression, and, in fact, the chord, which is to hold together the most disparate elements of the score, the tetrachord [0,2,5,8] or the half-diminished seventh (Ex. 10a). It has actually been heard a couple of times before, but only as an isolated colouring of a more than usually gruesome statement (Figs. 12/4, 21/3–23) or, later, apprehension (Fig. 206a/2); elsewhere it is employed as a fairly conventional II[7] (Fig. 69a/7). Its use here, however, is exceptionally interesting, as it gives the key to the set 6–30 and thus to Strauss's whole conception of musical language in *Elektra*, for, as it happens, this is one of those extraordinary moments in Strauss's music where one recognises plainly the source of his inspiration: it is a direct, if simplified, quotation from *Tristan*, indeed, from one of the most powerful harmonic ideas in that work (Ex. 10b). The relevance of the quotation is at this point not made clear, as in this section Strauss's version is treated as another much repeated harmonic formula, but at Fig. 177/7, its half-diminished seventh having been appropriated mid-pattern as a sort of blurred dominant to B minor (Fig. 176/10), Klytämnestra's bitonal aria is heralded by a new form of the chord whose role could not be more explicit (Exx. 10c and d).

Example 10a

138/3

Example 10b

Example 10c

Perhaps the most fascinating thing about this is the fact that Strauss, in transporting Wagner's idea to a new context in which the paired tetrachords are now resplit as [0,3,7]+[0,3,7], has not bothered to change the pitch (this is *the* definitive pitch of the *Tristan* chord). One of the more notable idiosyncrasies of his musical style in general is his pitch specificity: however chromatic or dissonant the surface, the key signature and, somewhere round the edges of the structure, the key remain. This tends to be equally true of his many borrowings. Likewise, there is often some correspondence of text and meaning, though the sense of the original may be distorted; here, one can see that the words match in a peculiarly warped, 'Expressionist' sort of fashion. While this is not the place to examine them in detail, Ex. 10b is hardly the only example from *Tristan* in *Elektra*, though it is probably the one whose consequences are the most far-reaching. Perhaps the most obvious aurally is the way the recognition aria draws unambiguously on 'Lausch, Geliebter!' (*Tristan*, Act II – beginning only a few bars later than and incorporating Ex. 10b), a passage whose continuing importance to him he was finally to acknowledge quite openly in *Metamorphosen* of 1943–5 (Ex. 11).

Example 11a

Example 11b

Example 11c

Of all nineteenth-century works *Tristan* must have had the most lasting influence on his music, an influence which became more, not less, profound; his letters make this very clear, and a sketch from 1946 (Ex. 12) demonstrates just how deeply he had understood 'what

Example 12

Strauss's condensation of *Tristan*, quoted by Krause, *Richard Strauss*, p. 90

[0,2,5,8]   [0,2,6,9]   [0,2,5,8]
7♯ 1st inversion   7♯ 1st inversion

Wagner put into it'.[16] In the symphonic poems and in *Salome*, still overcome by the sound of Wagner's music, this influence is expressed to a great extent as a matter of gesture and texture; though his talent for graphic (non-diatonic) depiction of perverted sentiment has without question already invaded *Salome*, much of it still depends – and the contrast is a large part of its effectiveness – on an uninhibited outpouring of sheer sonority. In *Elektra*, however, while there are moments of unadulterated beauty they are now severely restricted, being reserved for brief alliterative flashes of nostalgia (Fig. 158a onwards, as Elektra, in wonder herself, describes to Orestes her former life), irony (Fig. 141/3: 'Die Götter! bist doch selber eine Göttin! bist, was sie sind!' ['The gods! But you yourself are a goddess, you are like them!']) or insincerity (Elektra's seduction of Chrysothemis – compare Salome's beguiling sweetness with Narraboth): it is almost as if such music is no longer entirely real to Strauss either. Only at the recognition aria, where Elektra for a little while lets down her defences and the tension drops, can he indulge his more natural inclination – in a section of the libretto that he himself had asked to be inserted, as if it were hardly possible to keep up with Elektra's previously unremitting duty to a preordained fate – to wallow in the beauty of sound for its own sake. And yet when he does so even this has become a thinly disguised pastiche. One gets the faint but unmistakable impression that Strauss had reached the point where full-blown Wagnerian Romanticism had, while losing none of its hold over him, suddenly shifted as a compositional reality from the present to the past, a shift no doubt prompted by the demands of Hofmannsthal's uncompromisingly (neo-)classical text and initiating the process of gradual detachment and retrospection which colours to some degree all his music written after *Elektra*. Instead, most of his compositional attention focused on the structural possibilities implied by *Tristan*'s material – material he had not used before – rather than its style.

Returning, then to Fig. 177, we find that [0,2,5,8] or 4–27, the *Tristan* chord, is the binding agent between – or, in other words, a subset of – the tritonally related keys of B minor and F minor. Already familiar from its repetitive appearances in the Ex. 10a sequence which came to a climax at Fig. 174/8 as II ('Lass mich allein mit ihr!') and formed the transition to V, it has now loosened the confines of the sequence and opens the way to Klytämnestra's bitonal set 6–30. This established, her music diversifies, but 4–27 returns pointedly at other moments of transition, exploiting its inherent tonal ambivalence and thus providing a vital link either between tonality and bitonality or, just as importantly, between dissonant and diatonic sections (Ex. 13) – contrasted procedures he could only oppose in *Salome*. Here, his resources increased, Strauss could manage all types of transition

Example 13a

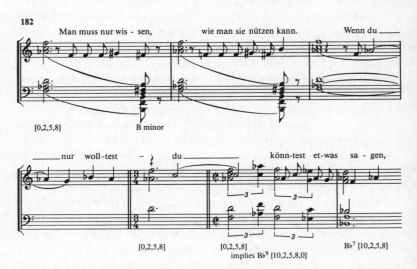

Example 13b

with great skill. Consider, for instance, how the dissonant F sharp/ G flat is gradually worked out of the introduction to the recognition aria (see Chapter 5, Ex. 7) and is only afterwards, in the coda, explained as a Tristanesque passing inflection – as part of [0,2,5,8] – on the dominant (Fig. 154a/2). This is one of the most satisfactory solutions in the whole opera. As an extension of this pivotal function, Strauss on occasion uses 4–27 not as a linking subset or, primarily, as a tonal chord but rather, playing on its ability to behave like neither one nor the other, as a means of temporarily disrupting a fundamentally diatonic section. At Fig. 166a, where, in her recitation to Orestes, the sense of Elektra's words changes briefly, [0,2,5,8] is prolonged through six bars of uncertain and meandering counterpoint before she resumes with 'Diese süssen Schauder' and it is understood as part of a large-scale Phrygian cadence to A major. Aegisthus' apprehensive 'Was hast du in der Stimme?' (Fig. 206a/2) is similar; both allow it to imply, for a short time, the imminent breakdown of diatonicism as the prevailing musical background.

The half-diminished seventh is thus exceptionally versatile, its tritone permitting it both to undermine and yet ultimately to accentuate the steadiness of such backgrounds, unreliable enough at the best of times in much of Strauss's music, and to lead naturally into regions themselves unstable. Klytämnestra's chord 6–30, its superset, might then be described as the pinnacle of instability, for it contains not one but three independent tritones. These admit of reinterpretation not merely as the two interlocking half-diminished sevenths, intersecting (in the minor) around the inner tritone (as in Ex. 10c), but also in a number of other interesting ways, of which Strauss took full advantage. One of the most useful of these is produced by combining that inner tritone with one of the outer versions (in minor, the root), giving the tetrachord [0,2,6,8] or 4–25. Like 4–27, 4–25 has a potentially crucial double function, for it may easily be assimilated into a tonal context as a French sixth, but may equally well provoke excursions into the previously unbounded territories of the wholetone scale. As the former, it has a jarring attack associated either with Klytämnestra's attendants (Figs. 143/3, 154/4) or, particularly, with Agamemnon's axe, whose disjointed chopping motive is one of Strauss's more disagreeably literal efforts (Figs. 67, 243, 45a onwards). Normally it will resolve as expected (Fig. 157/7), but it may intrude raucously as a direct reference to the axe's use into contrasted *milieux*, as at Fig. 117/2, where Elektra screams of murder. At Figs. 42–4, when at the height of her frenzied recollection of Agamemnon's death she predicts his wounded shade returning for vengeance – a passage inserted with horribly unequivocal effect at Fig. 197 (with Elektra's motive) into Klytämnestra's 'immer noch die Fackel vor der Tür, die grässlich zuckt, wie ein Lebendiges, und meinen Schlaf belauert' ('still the torch before the door, that flickers horribly, like a living thing, and spies on my sleep') – though he eventually treats the chord as an altered V of C minor to the rising octaves which will, at last, avenge her father in the furiously distorted dissonance of Fig. 192a/5, [0,2,6,8] begins in its insistence to push outside its tonal boundaries. Indeed, Elektra's sheer horror at the image of his being dragged headfirst and bleeding from the bath has already caused her music to lose all sense of tonal base, as at Fig. 41 [0,2,6,8] slithers in parallel motion, rising to the accented repetitions of Fig. 42 as her fear is contained and redirected towards its purpose at Fig. 44. At Fig. 72, her intense frustration that Chrysothemis' whispered tidings from Klytämnestra should have been heard through the door prompts another uncontrolled outburst, now starkly outlining the interval [0,6]; even the uncomplicated and hopeful Chrysothemis herself is sucked down into shifting panic at Fig. 98 as she realises that the effects of the deed will not spare her either. But it was Klytämnestra's deed, and it is really her music, touching the sisters only in so far as it deflects them from their different objects; neither Elektra's chord (of which [0,2,6,8] is not a subset) nor Chrysothemis' resolute E flat major is fundamentally shaken by it. For Klytämnestra, on the other hand, in a bitonal context only tenuously held together by the ambiguous half-diminished seventh, [0,2,6,8] serves altogether to undermine the comparative – if schizophrenic – sanity of 6–30. Sometimes the disintegration into parallel French sixths will afford only a brief glimpse of the sickness lurking beneath her outward composure (as at Fig. 172/2, where there is a slow and subtle decay from diatonicism through the Ex. 10a sequence into two bars of oscillating [0,2,6,8]s – for the word 'Eiterndes' ('pus') – and out again),[17] but in the central part of the scene (Figs. 186–93) her self-control vanishes and 4–25 spreads like the invisible blanket of terror which oppresses her over the musical texture, growing into fuller whole-tone clusters ([0,2,4,6,8] or 5–33) and, despite the intermittent imposition of some sort of order (such as the Ex. 5 sequence or the A pedal in the bass from Figs. 189 to 191/4), forcing her to cross the border into atonality. The complexity of the cadence at Fig. 193 (Ex. 8), after which comes the calmer, if uneasy, equilibrium of 6–30 and the heavy relief of 'Und dann schlaf ich', could then perhaps be understood as symbolic of the almost overwhelming difficulty she has in pulling herself out of her self-tormenting trauma: the E flat, from 5–33, *will* not, until the last minute, be shaken off.

However, despite the encroaching modernity of this passage, its significance is not that it sounds more or less atonal or whole-tone but that the source of its apparent atonality is in fact tonal. As distinct from its use in *Salome*, where Herod's sliding whole-tone scales could only add a decorative gloss to the underlying C major, now [0,2,6,8], while no less evocative of the mental imbalance they both portray, is (like [0,2,5,8]) held firmly in check by its relationship to 6–30, a set itself both implicative and closed. Because of this relationship (and the safety net of its own double meaning) Strauss is freer to dispense with the obvious trappings of tonality while retaining perfect control over this freedom: the music is thus paradoxically both modern and conventionally coherent.

Elektra's set 5–32 is, as one might expect, treated in a similar way. Again Strauss extracts a subset with its own tonal function, but here, because her bitonal keys are major instead of minor, this subset, in pointed opposition to those of Klytämnestra, serves to underline the assertiveness of her character, confirming rather than detracting from the certainty with which she pursues her aim. And yet it may also be seen to provide the link between the two women's otherwise unconnected 'nexus' sets, for Elektra's subset is as well as the psychological inverse the musical inversion of Klytämnestra's elusive [0,2,5,8], the dominant seventh or [0,2,6,9]. These two forms are actually juxtaposed in Ex. 10a (last bar), but there one's attention is always drawn to the accented and less stable form and [0,2,6,9] does not resolve as a V⁷; indeed, Klytämnestra's scene is remarkable for its total lack of definite dominants, [0,2,5,8] tending to stand in – logically enough – as a substitute. Quite the reverse is true of Elektra's music. That the positive form of the set is unquestionably hers is clear from the very spacing of [0,1,4,6,9] (or, more accurately, [0,1,4,7,9] in the major), which, though retaining the B and not C flat spelling, separates the E from the upper part of the chord, a V⁷ in $\frac{4}{2}$ position (see Ex. 2). Its immediate dissolution onto an E major $\frac{4}{2}$ echoes this, and [0,2,6,9] makes several isolated and colouristic appearances in the following section (for instance, Fig. 8/5). But though this is not inappropriate to the introductory and relatively simple first scene, Strauss must at once have realised that, however often or noisily he used it, [0,2,6,9] (like [0,3,6,9] or the diminished seventh, another subset of 6-30 which Strauss just about completely ignores as too normative for Klytämnestra) could not in itself be sufficiently emphatic or complicated a sonority either to be easily assimilable into Elektra's predominantly thick and dissonant textures or to allow any real – and therefore productive – ambivalence of interpretation. For, unlike [0,2,5,8] or [0,2,6,8], [0,2,6,9] continues to sound pretty much like a V⁷ whatever its circumstances.

So instead Strauss has chosen a different approach: the integrative foil to Elektra's chord is not a subset of [0,1,4,6,9] but, as becomes evident in the introduction to her aria (Figs. 34/12–36/5), its complement, the set 7–32, which is given literally in answer to Elektra's [5,4,1,11,8] as [6,7,9,10,0,2,3], filling in all twelve notes (cf. Ex. 4b). But what is most remarkable about this statement of 7–32 is not just its pitches, which are suggestive enough in themselves, but their arrangement, for Strauss has characteristically presented the set in tonal form as the dominant minor thirteenth. He is thus able at one go both to neutralise her dissonance and to incorporate its subset [0,2,6,9] as part of a more extended V whose role is not in doubt but which allows him considerably more scope for alternative segmentations. As we have seen, dominant chords have a strongly articulative function throughout the work, whether as the Ex. 4b progression or elsewhere. In the diatonic sections or those in an undisturbed major mode, [0,2,6,9] may in fact suffice alone, generally well prepared by chromatic sequence (Fig. 247a), by solid harmonic support (Figs. 228a–30a as I–II⁷–V⁷–I or Figs. 107–9 as I⁶–VI–II⁷–V⁷–I – here the sheer exuberance of the diatonicism seems to have got out of hand) or simply by orchestral reinforcement (for instance, Fig. 129a/2, where after Elektra's 'Kannst du nicht die Botschaft austrompeten' ['Can you not blare out your message'], indisputably in D minor but during the course of which the bass line seems to have been lost, the independent strands reconverge with full orchestral support on V at her reference to Orestes). But where the mode or key is less plain it is striking that, though the dominant is no less persistent or intelligible as such, Strauss will always adopt a version of 7–32.[18] At its most forceful this is usually V♭9 or 5–31, [0,1,3,6,9] (a chord just hinted at in passing at Figs. 35/3 and 36), either as an incisive agent of modulation (Fig. 256) or to give a point of clarity within a passage tonally unpredictable (as at Fig. 123/5, where its penetrating distinctness endows it with a clear definitive power). V♭13 itself may similarly add definition to the end of a short non-diatonic sequence (Fig. 40: [0,2,6,8]–[0,3,6,9]–[0,2,6,9]–V♭13), but it is inherently less categorical a dominant than V♭9 and Strauss instead prefers to stress its ability without losing its implicit will to sound like one to propagate new, and especially whole-tone, sets. It is frequently reduced to the bare outlines of V as [0,2,4,8], as at Fig. 139/3; here (and for the refrain 'sie hat geträumt' at Fig. 119/4) it retains the root, but it may also appear in a less obvious configuration (Fig. 184/9) or, indeed, using this latter motive, be simplified into the equal-interval [0,4,8], as in Ex. 9e(ii). It is this set that moves across into Klytämnestra's music to supply most of the motivation (as in Ex. 9f) for her more transitory sections, otherwise – despite [0,2,5,8] – predominantly static and repetitive, providing, in as ambiguous a manner as possible, a much-needed cadential formula – significantly, in a form which cannot conflict stylistically with her own whole-tone subset [0,2,6,8]. Conversely, the reduction to such amorphous fragments of 7–32 demonstrates that aurally at least Elektra, in her borrowings of 4–25 and frantic use of other tritonal material (as at Fig. 120a/4, where she is startled by Orestes' entrance into a darting motive describing [0,2,6]), is perhaps not as remote from her mother's fears as her contradictory inversion of 4–27 would suggest.

In his complementation of [0,1,4,6,9] Strauss has thus brought under his complete structural control one of the most fundamental chord complexes of all tonal music. During the first half of the opera its employment becomes more and more diverse, growing from the opening [0,2,6,9] of Elektra's chord into V^{b13} and thence breaking down at the height of Klytämnestra's delirium into looser particles, abstracted shadows of its former confidence. But as Elektra moves towards her goal and her confidence returns, so is 7–32 resimplified to V^7 in preparation for the final denouement. This is particularly obviously displayed in the Ex. 9e(iii) motive at Fig. 200a/3, where Elektra greets Aegisthus: now – though the melodic outline is identical – the B flat is no longer treated as part of a V^{b13} but resolves quite unambiguously as a dominant seventh (in its original $^4_2$ position), just as [0,1,4,6,9] itself has done at Fig. 199a (cf. Ex. 4e). Even the subversive [0,4,8] associated with this motive is now safely incorporated into Aegisthus' material as an altered tonic; Ex. 9f has been altogether abandoned. A little earlier, in the section before she recognises her brother (Fig. 123a onwards), [0,4,8] and 7–32 still persist to haunt the weary Elektra, but even here they are safely enclosed, [0,4,8] by the confines of the chordal announcement of Orestes' arrival (Ex. 9d) and V^{b13} by an undeniably crude circle of fifths at Fig. 134a ([0,2,4,8]–[0,1,3,7,9], or a form of V^{b11}). Indeed, these joint processes of containment and clarification affect all types of dissonance, as if Strauss at Fig. 1a has consciously and deliberately decided to reverse his compositional procedure. [0,2,5,8] and [0,2,6,8] return – if heard at all – to their illustrative duties or, as already noted, to specifically tonal contexts. Klytämnestra's bitonal set 6–30 makes no further impression, emerging only for a fleeting instant before she dies. On the contrary, the continued 'modernity' of some of the second half is on the whole due not to an addition to diatonicism but to a *subtraction* from it, usually in the form of a misplaced bass (as in the passage cited above), often accompanied by a new reliance on a vague and distracted counterpoint. Only Elektra's fury and determination continue unabated, at last subsiding onto a mild diminished seventh as she herself collapses (Fig. 260a/4).

III

So, a structure whose procedures are mirrored in themselves, exactly matching the dramatic form in their expansion into complexity and out again and in which one, at least, of the original bitonal sets is 'neutralised'. But what, if anything, constitutes large-scale resolution? Why, to come back to the key structure, does the work end with the juxtaposition of E flat minor and C minor/major? A psychological explanation of Strauss's various tonalities, however convincing, can be only half the answer; likewise, despite their obvious framing function, it seems unlikely, given the unusual coherence with which the surface appears to be held together, that such tonalities can have been chosen in an altogether arbitrary or external fashion. Here one finds a solution in Strauss's most unexpected and ingenious exploitation of the nature of bitonal complementation.

It so happens that he has chosen to make use of only those combinations which fulfil certain very interesting conditions (see Table 1). First, they must, reasonably enough, contain as subsets one or other of the quasi-tonal tetrachords 4–25 and 4–27 (the latter either in its *Tristan* or in its dominant-seventh form) and preferably both. In fact only Klytämnestra's set 6–30 includes 4–25 at all; of the rest, a large number are immediately cut out for want of 4–27, leaving 5–32, 5–34, 6-Z28, 6-Z29, 6–33, 6-Z50 and again 6–30. 5–34, 6-Z28 and 6-Z50 contain both inversions of 4–27. Secondly, in keeping with Strauss's prevailing textures, they must be neither related by diatonic interval nor major in effect, presumably because the resulting relationship would have been judged too obvious or insufficiently complex for comfort. As a consequence, most of the five- and two of the six-member sets are removed from the running, including the potentially useful 5–34 (V^9) and 6–33 (V^{11}). Only 6-Z29, C minor and D major, which may be presented as $V^{11}_{\flat 9}$, slips through this particular net. But thirdly, and most importantly, the two triads of Strauss's bitonal chords must have as their complement a set which either spells out or has embedded within it a second bitonal pair. Thus, the set 6–20 – C minor and E major, [11,0,3,4,7,8] or [0,1,4,5,8,9] – is complemented by [10,9,6,5,2,1], or F sharp minor and B flat major. In the case of the self-complementary six-member sets, this process is fairly straightforward, and 6–20, 6–30, 6–32 and 6–33 all comply. Of the Z-related hexachords, 6-Z26 and 6-Z28 do not, and 6-Z19's complement 6-Z44 is only explicable in (bi-)tonal terms through a rather contrived coupling of relative major and minor; but 6-Z50 and 6-Z29 prove the ideal counterpart for each other. It is notable, incidentally, that the roots of the four or six triads produced by these means all fall on notes of the whole-tone and not the diatonic or semitonal scale.[19] The four- and five-member sets, on the other hand, naturally incorporate within their larger complements an embedded version of themselves, often overlapping with one or more transposi-

Table 1

	Subsets 4-25/4-27	Non-diatonic roots	Bitonal complement
C major/D♭ major — [8,7,5,4,10] [0,1,3,4,7,8] — 6-Z19 I_8	–	√	–
C minor/D♭ minor — [0,1,3,4,7,8] — 6-Z19 t0	–	√	–
C major/D♭ minor — [0,1,4,7,8] — 5-22 t0	–	√	7-22 D major/E♭ minor + B♭ major/B minor
C minor/D♭ major — [0,1,3,5,7,8] — 6-Z26 $t0/I_8$	–	√	–
C major/D major — [9,7,6,4,2,0] [0,2,3,5,7,9] — 6-33 I_9	[0,2,6,9] t0	–	A♭ minor/B♭ minor
C minor/D minor — [0,2,3,5,7,9] — 6-33 t0	[0,2,5,8] t7	–	E major/F♯ major
C major/D minor — [0,2,4,5,7,9] — 6-32 t0	–	–	A♭ minor/F♯ major
C minor/D major — [6,7,9,0,2,3] [0,1,3,6,8,9] — 6-Z29 t6	[0,2,6,9] t0 [0,2,5,8] t7	– $(V_{\flat 9}^{11})$	E minor/B♭ major
C major/E♭ major — [4,3,0,10,7] [0,1,4,6,9] — 5-32 I_4	[0,2,6,9] t10	√	7-32 D minor/B minor + [1,8]

Table 1 (*cont.*)

				Subsets 4-25/4-27	Non-diatonic roots	Bitonal complement
	C minor/Eb minor	[6,7,10,0,3] [0,1,4,6,9]	5-32 t6	[0,2,5,8] t10	–	7-32 Db major/E major +[2,9]
	C major/Eb minor	[3,4,6,7,10,0] [0,1,3,4,7,9]	6-Z28 t3	[0,2,6,9] t10 [0,2,5,8] t10	√	–
	C minor/Eb major	[7,10,0,3] [0,3,5,8]	4-26 t7/I3	–	–	8-26 A minor/F# major + D major/ B minor+E minor/G major
	C major/E major	[0,11,8,7,4] [0,1,4,5,8]	5-21 I0	–	–	7-21 D major/F# major/Bb major +[3]
	C minor/E minor	[4,3,0,11,7] [0,1,4,5,8]	5-21 t11	–	√	7-21 D minor/F# minor/Bb minor +[8]
	C major/E minor	[0,11,7,4] [0,1,5,8]	4-20 t11	–	–	8-20 D major/F# minor +F# major/Bb minor +Bb major/D minor
	C minor/E major	[11,0,3,4,7,8] [0,1,4,5,8,9]	6-20 t11	–	√	F# minor/Bb major
	C major/F major	[4,5,7,9,0] [0,1,3,5,8]	5-27 t4	–	–	7-27 B major+F# major +[2,8]

Table 1 (cont.)

				Subsets 4-25/4-27	Non-diatonic roots	Bitonal complement
	C minor/F minor	[8,7,5,3,0] [0,1,3,5,8]	5-27 I_8	—	—	7-27 B minor + F♯ minor + [4,10]
	C major/F minor	[4,5,7,8,0] [0,1,3,4,8]	5-Z17 t4	—	—	7-Z17 F♯ major + B minor + [3,9]
	C minor/F major	[3,5,7,9,0] [0,2,4,6,9]	5-34 t3	[0,2,6,9] t3 [0,2,5,8] t7	—	7-34 B minor/E major + D♭ minor/G♭ major
	C major/F♯ major	[7,6,4,1,0,10] [0,1,3,6,7,9]	6-30 I_7	[0,2,6,8] t4 [0,2,6,9] t10 [0,2,6,8] t10	√	D minor/A♭ minor
	C minor/F♯ minor	[0,1,3,6,7,9]	6-30 t0	[0,2,5,8] t1 [0,2,5,8] t7 [0,2,6,8] t7	√	B♭ major/E major
	C major/F♯ minor	[0,1,4,6,7,9]	6-Z50 t0	[0,2,5,8] t4 [0,2,6,9] t7	√	D minor/E major
	C minor/F♯ major	[6,7,10,0,1,3] [0,1,4,6,7,9]	6-Z50 t6	[0,2,5,8] t10 [0,2,6,9] t1	√	A♭ minor/B♭ major

tions; the placement of their roots may vary considerably. All three of these factors having been taken into account, Strauss is then left with a remarkably small and unified group of possible bitonal chords, comprising 5–32, 6–30, 6-Z50 and 6-Z29. The two former sets are of course precisely those which, making use of their versatility within the first two categories, have been seen to dominate the musical action; it is, as one might expect, through the third that they extend their influence a little distance into the background.

It has often been wondered what connection Elektra's chord could have with the tonal structure: E major is heard only at moments of extreme joy, and D flat major is not used at all; indeed, in spite of its manifest integration through its dominant subset, its independence is part of its effectiveness. But Salome's dissonant superimposition is finally resolved (in her case, as a cadence), and Elektra, too, comes to some sort of peace. Here, however, her resolution takes the form of a sudden dull collapse – after the neutral diminished seventh mentioned above – onto E flat minor and C minor, both of which have come to be associated with death (see Ex. 14). But now their brutal

Example 14

Example 4 (*cont.*)

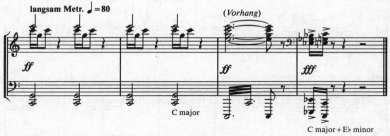

juxtaposition signifies more than an unusually unpleasant double dose, as it were; rather, it explains it, for this is the complementary opposition to her positive D flat major/E major, the dark side of Elektra's character and the fate which, implicit if unstated within her assertive $V^{\flat 13}$ from the moment she speaks, she is unable to avoid. The agonising wrench that returns the key to her C major[20] and to the savage *fff* fanfare – with E flat minor – with which the opera ends might then be considered a curious and spiteful gesture, because though C major has been her symbol of triumph this bitonal combination, 6-Z28, is the only possible one which, though obeying the first and second preconditions for its use, flaunts the third: it has no tonal complement, and is therefore indissoluble – a suitably twisted and 'Expressionist' negation of the validity of Elektra's *Tod durch Verklärung*. This chord has, in fact, been heard once before, at what is, in effect, the turning point of the whole work, when Elektra, *aufschreiend*, recognises Orestes at Fig. 144a (Ex. 15).[21] Here, sus-

Example 15

144a

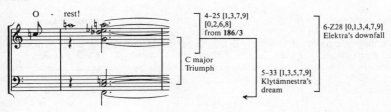

pended over F and in an arrangement whose conflicting implications could not express more clearly her own mixed feelings,[22] 6-Z28 discloses before she has even realised it herself that her ambitions are already irredeemably tainted from within; their realisation, not fully comprehended until the last bar, can only be a partial resolution. Nonetheless, she does better than Klytämnestra, unstable from the start. Her bitonal B minor/F minor could have been complemented by A major and E flat major, but she is permitted no such release from her terrors. On the contrary, they prove to be justified, for Strauss allows Elektra, in another violent proclamation of intent (when, at Fig. 11a, she refuses absolutely to believe that Orestes will not come (see Chapter 7, Ex. 8)), to appropriate this tritone in the form of her own superset 6-Z50 and thus to become the agent of her mother's death.

Finally, one can see how this tendency to complementation clarifies aspects of the overall tonal organisation. Focusing again on Elektra, it now becomes clear that not only does her chord determine its own final outcome but also 6-Z50, as its more dramatic extension, may equally have its own and less specific role. This is perhaps made most apparent in the way Scenes 2 and 6 relate, for, confirming one's impression that the opera is in some sense mirrored about its central (symmetrical) axis, Elektra's transition from B flat minor to C major during the course of her monologue, which may be represented as 6-Z29, is exactly reflected in the total contrast between Orestes' tense D minor and the calm of her A flat major, keys which spell out 6-Z50. Thus, in a balance of opposites not attainable by the too sharply defined 5–32, Strauss's desire for perfection of frame is pulled together with his desire for perfection of internal structure (Table 2: cf. Ex. 1).

Table 2

1 INTRODUCTION 5–32 Db major/E major: Elektra's chord	2	3	4	5	6	7 RESOLUTION 5–32
	6-Z29 Bb minor → Eb C major		6–30 B minor/ F minor	Eb	6-Z50 D minor → Ab major	Eb minor/C minor: Elektra's death

7 Elektra's voice: music and language in Strauss's opera

CAROLYN ABBATE

Do I hear the music? The music comes from me.[1]

I

Hearing, not hearing, hearing lies, silence: the opera *Elektra* is a play upon sounds, voices and music itself, a play upon the collected utterances of its characters. This obsession with hearing was latent in Hofmannsthal's play; the questions 'hört ihr das?', 'hörst du's nicht?' ('Do you hear that?', 'Don't you hear it?'), the injunction 'hör mich!' ('listen!'), the cry 'ich will's nicht hören' ('I don't want to hear it') tumble obsessively from the mouth of every character, as if the line of Atreus were distinguished not by a characteristic nose or slant of eye, but by this inescapable linguistic tic. Even Aegisthus, living too long in their midst, adopts it in his last moments; his 'Hört mich niemand?' ('Does no one hear me?') is answered: 'Agamemnon hört dich!' ('Agamemnon hears you!'). As Elektra speaks, we know her stepfather goes to a realm to whose conversation the living are not privy. Chrysothemis is a virtuoso in reporting what she has heard; listening to secrets at the door, she catches Aegisthus' schemes against Elektra: 'Sie werfen dich in einen Turm, wo du von Sonn' und Mond das Licht nicht sehen wirst. Sie tun's, ich weiss es, ich hab's gehört' ('They will throw you into a tower, where you'll never see the light of sun or moon again. They'll do it, I know, I heard').

Most importantly, the Elektra–Klytämnestra scene is set spinning by the sound of a voice. Elektra's sudden, honeyed address, 'Die Götter! bist doch selber eine Göttin! bist, was sie sind' ('The gods! but you yourself are a goddess! you are what they are'), startles Klytämnestra into an urgent twofold question: 'Habt ihr gehört? habt ihr verstanden, was sie redet?' ('Did you hear that? did you understand what she said?'). Klytämnestra here calls into question

the honoured bond between hearing and understanding, the idea
that the truth of words is divined by listening:

> Listening is . . . linked (in a thousand varied, indirect forms) to a hermeneutics:
> to listen is to adopt an attitude of decoding what is obscure, blurred, or
> mute, in order to make available to consciousness the 'underside' of meaning
> . . . The communication postulated by this second listening is religious: it
> ligatures the listening subject to the hidden world of the gods, who, as every-
> one knows, speak a language of which only a few enigmatic fragments reach
> men, though it is vital – cruelly enough – for them to understand this
> language.[2]

Barthes' formulation might well stand as warning. Klytämnestra
rightly doubts the possibility of 'decoding what is obscure', for
much of what is heard in *Elektra* consists of messages that block
meaning and mislead the listener. Elektra's cruel game with listening
and truth in her confrontation with Klytämnestra is one where she
describes to an avid listener – one who shouts 'rede doch', 'gib mir
Antwort' ('speak', 'answer me') – the sacrificial victim and the rituals
that will purge Klytämnestra of her dreams. Elektra speaks to dilate
time before revealing the truth – that the victim described *is* Klytämnestra – and Klytämnestra misinterprets, hearing soothing words
from a repentant child. The play's supreme falsehood, the report of
Orestes' death, is only the loudest and gaudiest of the lot.

A text so charged with signals for sound and voice seems almost
predestined to become opera; certainly Strauss was struck by its
potential immediately, upon first seeing the play.[3] This is not to say
that Hofmannsthal had, fortuitously, created a libretto, incomplete
if taken without music; in *Literaturoper* music does not finish something left unexecuted (which is the case with conventional libretti
and with Wagner's dramatic poems, both contrived for musical
setting).[4] Strauss's musical setting greatly amplified *Elektra*'s latent
obsession with hearing, not by making alterations to the text – alterations *were* of course made for other reasons – but rather by using
music itself as a series of voices, as a teller of stories. Music in
Elektra becomes a kind of indirect discourse, at times a representation of the characters' words in another language, at times the voice
of an outsider, a narrator, at times the voice of music *en pur*: this is
operatic music polyphonic not in the usual sense, but in a Bakhtinian
sense of having many different tongues or languages.[5]

At times, however, the music has one voice, more direct than the
others: Elektra's voice. In this context, the critical text is a brief
remark near the end of the play, as Chrysothemis asks the question
about 'hearing' one last time, and Elektra responds:

CHRYSOTHEMIS   . . . alle
umarmen sich, und jauchzen, tausend Fackeln
sind angezündet. Hörst du nicht, so hörst du
denn nicht?
ELEKTRA   Ob ich nicht höre? ob ich die
Musik nicht höre? sie kommt doch aus mir
heraus.[6]
CHRYSOTHEMIS . . . they are all embracing one another and
rejoicing. A thousand torches have been lit.
Don't you hear it? Don't you hear it?
ELEKTRA   Don't I hear it? Do I hear the music? The
music comes from me.

Who is this Elektra, that she answers a question about embraces,
shouts of joy and torches by saying that she hears music, music that
'comes from me'? In Hofmannsthal's play, as in the opera, this is the
sole reference to music, and anyone attuned to Strauss's autobiographical preoccupations with operatic characters who are composers
(manifest in the Prologue to *Ariadne auf Naxos* and in *Capriccio*)
would expect that this text might represent some cardinal moment in
Elektra. But that detail is perhaps less important than the abyss that
opens, for the opera, under Elektra's words. What we hear at the end
of the opera is music Elektra not only *hears* (for her, Chrysothemis'
question is ludicrous, and 'ob ich die Musik nicht höre' has an in-
credulous, ironic tinge that is hard to render in English), it is music
she has *created*, a sonorous world which is her thought, loosed
upon us.

Elektra's words, in short, undermine a conventional operatic
illusion, that operatic characters do not hear the music in which they
speak and which surrounds them. The impression that music in
opera is an outside voice, with its own integrity, commenting on and
projecting the stage drama, is one aptly summarised by Edward T.
Cone, who distinguishes between the 'vocal protagonist', embodied
in the human voice and the character, and an implicit or 'complete
musical persona':

The complete musical persona . . . is a projection of [the composer's]
musical intelligence, constituting the mind, so to speak, of the composition
in question . . . The typical protagonist, we remember, is assumed to be
actually unconscious of singing. Not so the implicit musical persona, which
is always aware of both words and music; the musical persona is an
intelligence in the act of thinking through words and music alike.[7]

Elektra becomes in Cone's terms both vocal protagonist and the
'mind of the composition'; or, rather, the music is a composition that
resounds inside her mind. Strauss's *Elektra* thus pushes at the fragile

barriers that separate any of us from the mind of another; perhaps this accounts in part for its force.

Elektra's words – 'the music comes from me' – confirm her status as true hero and protagonist of the opera, a status sometimes denied by what can only be called formidably masculine readings of the opera. But beyond this, the words also hint at a richer hearing of Strauss's music, not as the stolid, monolithic utterance of the composer, but as music whose tonal language, vocabulary, degree of fusion with words, may shift fluidly to accommodate many different voices.

II

This is the first musical voice in the opera (see Ex. 1). That this is an 'Agamemnon' motive is a truism, yet also a misreading, one whose boundaries are wide: on the one hand, entrenched notions about

Example 1

what motives can mean; on the other, the question of Agamemnon's presence in the opera. Richard Specht's essay on *Elektra* (1921), one of the first extended analyses of the work, described the 'prelude of the opera, [consisting] of three bars of the Agamemnon theme, which, like an heraldic crest mounted upon a mighty lintel, stands over our entry to the whole'.[8] The notion that the whole work is subsumed under a sign for Agamemnon has comforting (if rather vague) suggestions of musical unity; Specht was, of course, led to argue that this dominating, overarching paterfamilias is evoked whenever the motive sounds. Whether by design or coincidence, Kurt Overhoff, in his book devoted to the opera, also described the 'Agamemnon' motive in the rugged language of structural engineering: 'Like the arched gateway of the palace at Mycenae . . . so the gloomy triadic arpeggiation of the death key D minor, the Agamemnon motive, at once musical motto and leitmotive, arches up in primeval nobility over the score'.[9] Overhoff went on to contrast the 'Agamemnon' motive with the so-called 'Elektra' chord (the sonority that opens her monologue), characterising the latter as shapeless, pure flaccid sonority without rhythmic or thematic character to give it sharp edges, and symbolising the passive emptiness of Elektra. Elektra seems no more than a vessel to contain mourning, the tain of a mirror that reflects Agamemnon: he is the 'true hero' of the opera.[10]

Feminist writers like Elaine Showalter, who describes critics who 'quietly transform . . . the novel into a male document',[11] might be taken aback by the roar with which Specht and Overhoff convert *Elektra* into an opera about Agamemnon, a roar that rivals the thunder of Strauss's most cacophonous orchestrations. Of course, Freudian accents can be discerned in any reading of Sophocles, Hofmannsthal or Strauss that luxuriates in speculations on Elektra's emptiness or impotence as the natural condition of women.[12] But while we might derive no little merriment from the robust metaphors in which Overhoff couches his descriptions (Elektra chord passive and 'motionless', Agamemnon motive 'arching up' above), the homocentric reading, in so far as it impinges on matters of musical interpretation, demands some response. And while we may well agree broadly with the anti-leitmotivic plaint made by Arnold Whittall, that interpretation of operatic music should not become obsessed with 'translatable meaning',[13] we need to be aware that operatic music rarely speaks in one voice and that the semiotic voice of motivic encoding may be one among the many.

What is the true significance of the opera's opening gesture? Its identification as 'signifying Agamemnon' rests, of course, upon Elektra's sung statement of the motive to her father's name, as, for example, at the opening of her monologue; the rhythm and contour of the motive, as Specht pointed out,[14] are calculated as a musical tracing of the name's intonation and scansion. This is a typical Straussian gambit; the 'Keikobad' motive in *Die Frau ohne Schatten* is another well-known instance. Loose Wagnerian habits have accustomed us to associate musical swatch and image in a straightforward way when motive and word join together in this fashion.

But we have been too swift in our dispensation of meaning. The thing for which the motive stands, in the classic semiotic sense,[15] is not Agamemnon at all, but rather Elektra's *voice*; more specifically, the mourning lament that so strongly marks her existence. In Hofmannsthal's play, the very first words, spoken by the serving maids, refer to Elektra not by her appearance but by her voice. She is inescapable din: 'Ist doch ihre Stunde, die Stunde wo sie um den Vater heult, dass alle Wände schallen' ('This is her time, the time when she wails for her father, and the walls themselves reverberate'). Hofmannsthal was here transposing into chattered commentary the famous initial gesture in Sophocles' play: Orestes' rounded prologue before the royal palace is interrupted when Elektra, invisible inside the house, begins to shriek. Her unarticulated mourning cry slashes across language and poetry, and, like the clangour of a great gong, sets the action moving in its course.

What Hofmannsthal muffled by transposition into indirect commentary – the serving maids only *describe* the wail – Strauss releases in his opening stroke. The wordless voice of the motive *is* Elektra's cry, and in the later melding of motive and word the orchestral cry of lament has merely become momentarily articulate and lingual. One could read the end of the opera – Elektra's silence and her mad dance, 'schweigen und tanzen' – as a reversal of the procedure, as the singer, in dying, surrenders her tongue back to music.

Rethinking the meaning of *Elektra*'s opening gesture brings with it, necessarily, a new understanding of recurrences of the motive, which saturates certain stretches of the score (for instance, Elektra's monologue, the Elektra–Orestes scene). Long experience with Wagner's works has taught us that even in the most lexical of his operas (the *Ring*) the referential meaning of motives is by no means immanent in the score. Rather, the motives may begin with specific associations, then quickly slide away from their symbolic nexus to become 'symphonic' or 'purely musical' matter; or they may begin as musical gestures and occasionally don masks of extramusical meaning. The four-note figure to which Sieglinde sings 'Du bist der Lenz' in *Die Walküre* is a complex instance of the latter, as within and after the 'Spring Song' the motive takes on and sheds texts to propose solutions to Siegmund's riddle about Brother Spring. These elaborate, specific associations for the motive are relevant nowhere else in the *Ring*.

The motives in *Elektra* are, to be sure, most often used 'symphonically', unburdened of their associations. But perhaps the dialectical extremes of 'extramusical sign' and 'symphonic device' are exaggeratedly separate in the case of the opening motive. As both a representation of voice and voice *qua* music it hovers between the two extremes. This fluidity is exploited by Strauss in the final moments of the recognition scene (Fig. 140a *et seq.*), where the motive undergoes a series of transformations (see Ex. 2). This is 'symphonic' metamorphosis in the classic Wagnerian manner: out of the extended two-voice canonic statement (a) the characteristic open-

Example 2

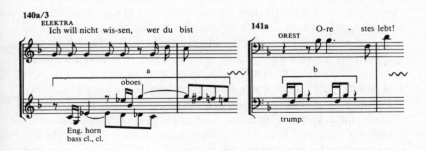

ing fourth is isolated (b), then reconverted into a fast, figural statement of the original form (c); in the final twist of the kaleidoscope
the motive is transformed into the so-called 'despair' motive (d), the
motto that opens the opera's second half with Chrysothemis' annunciation of Orestes' death. We need, perhaps, say no more about the
musical structure than that the entire sequence is part of a strong,
middle-range cadential progression which prepares the notoriously
dissonant (and loud) 'delayed' resolution to A flat preceding Elektra's
rhapsody to Orestes.

The conventional leitmotivic analysis of this passage views the
purported 'Agamemnon' motive as a critical clue in the drama of
recognition, in effect, as the composer's signal to us (unheard by the
characters) that this mysterious stranger is the missing male in
Agamemnon's brood.[16] The banality of this reading can have little
charm; yet must we retreat to flat musical description?

Regarding the motive as a representation of voice, on the other
hand, animates our hearing of the 'polyphony' in the recognition

drama. The motive ((a) in Ex. 2) is heard previously, during much of Elektra's and Orestes' exchanges, from the moment of Elektra's identification of herself: 'Ich bin das hündisch vergossene Blut des Königs Agamemnon: Elektra heiss ich' ('I am the cravenly outpoured blood of King Agamemnon: Elektra is my name'). The subsequent speeches for Elektra and Orestes are shadowed by marked thematic and orchestral alternations. The motive sounds in winds and strings, as a counterpoint to Elektra's words alone (five bars after Fig. 136a). Very different thematic matter, with brass sonorities, accompanies Orestes, until, at his 'Furchtbar sind deine Augen, hohl sind deine Wangen' ('Your eyes are terrible, your face is hollow'), the orchestra suddenly breaks the pattern of alternation and speaks instead in Elektra's voice (see Ex. 3).

Elektra, shut in upon herself, has not really heard Orestes' words, will not look at him; her speech is saturated with denials of her inter-locutor: 'lass mich', 'ich will nicht wissen, wer du bist, ich will nie-mand sehen' ('leave me alone', 'I don't want to know who you are, I wish to see no one'). This solipsistic discourse is mimicked by the musical discourse, the bald juxtaposition of her own monotonous, repetitive orchestral sentence with Orestes' musical voice, which cannot affect her music or deflect its course.

Example 3

Example 3 (*cont.*)

Yet if Elektra, possessed, does not hear the outsider, we know what she does hear, for we hear it with her: her own mourning voice, never stilled, until, in the passage shown in Ex. 3, it shrouds Orestes' very words with its noise. The musical fabric is thus not the 'voice' of an outside narrator, great with information, nor that of Cone's 'complete musical persona', but the trace of the music in Elektra's mind. In this 'polyphony' beyond mere counterpoint, the protagonist Elektra sings with representations of her Elektra-voice in the orchestra.

III

Lingering over *Elektra*'s opening motive is an indulgence in detail, yet also a tangential approach to an issue no less vexing than fundamental: the fusion of music and language in opera, or the clashes between them. The latter – the notion that music and words can be at odds – is still ill-served by opera criticism.[17] The former is a commonplace. That music in opera should project a 'drama' analogous to that projected by the words seems a precept so ordinary as to merit only a brief ceremonial curtsey before we rush to engage music analysis or *Librettistik*. But our ideas about music's connection to text and staged drama are, in many cases, simply those shopworn assumptions we inherited from Wagnerian exegeses of the nineteenth and early twentieth centuries, and we have not, on the whole, engaged the issue with the intelligence we routinely accord to musical matters.

The stock of our assumptions can be summarised rather briefly. Operatic music may have a self-evident capacity to symbolise textual elements through leitmotives or tonalities (D minor is the 'death key' in *Elektra*, as Overhoff put it). Carl Dahlhaus has pointed out that manipulations of formal conventions may serve dramatic purpose; the 'Spring Song' is a 'song' that loses its formal moorings under the pressures of the moment.[18] Yet most of us would find familiar another (putatively) Wagnerian blandishment, that operatic music has nonetheless a tonal, structural and thematic integrity which is coolly maintained through any obligations to symbolise words or stage action, attaining a symphonic state of grace.[19]

The cosiness of this vision – the eaten cake eternally restored to the plate, with operatic music at once expressing language and stage action, and 'working' as pure musical structure – does seem highly suspect in our current, more sceptical critical climate. For one thing, the voice of absolute music – music pursuing its own logic – may be a wilful voice, turning away from the meaning of text or the progress of the action on stage. More than this: operatic music may have aspirations beyond mere symphonic structure, and have means other than leitmotive, tonal symbol, formal transformation, for the symbolisation of textual elements and the projection of the drama.

In *Elektra* the authoritarian voice of the narrating 'leitmotivic' commentary is but rarely heard. Indeed, blatant leitmotivic passages are far fewer than in the *Ring*, and leitmotivists like Specht and William Mann (whose guide to Strauss's operas is a sort of lesser *Wagner Nights*) have gone far astray in their arduous labour of decoding. Where this commenting voice is relatively hushed, the drama is projected by other means.

Small-scale harmonic and linear choreographies that shadow twists of textual meaning are one of these. Wagner was, of course, master of this art and wrote of it, in characteristically opaque terms, in such credos as *Oper und Drama* and 'Über die Anwendung der Musik auf das Drama'. Strauss was hardly unique in adopting this Wagnerian custom; in the early twentieth century it was greatly honoured in the observance, by composers endowed more with the gentle lustre of idiosyncrasy than with the hot glow of originality (Puccini comes to mind). Strauss was merely the most Wagnerian in his colours.

A trio of related gestures will illustrate the point. In all three Elektra interrupts an interlocutor with a characteristic musical gesture, an intoning of the pitches A–D and a concomitant brush with the triad built on D. That Elektra's gesture is, clearly, related to the opera's opening bars (and the opening motive's emphasis on the A–D interval) is less remarkable than its changing import in several contexts.

In the first Elektra–Chrysothemis conversation, Chrysothemis' diatonic E flat 'waltz' ('Ich hab's wie Feuer in der Brust') is an evocation of womanly desires which Elektra, typically, hardly hears. Her murmured comment upon Chrysothemis' 'Hörst du mich an?' ('Are you listening?') is not an answer; 'Armes Geschöpf!' ('Poor creature!') has the air of an idle, familiar formula, expressing only absent-mindedness (see Ex. 4). In this cadential line (in an E flat

Example 4

major context), Elektra's interpolated A–D, and the supporting harmony, are barely disjunctive, a passing phenomenon smoothly integrated into the linear and harmonic progress of the passage. Whatever small frisson of awryness is engendered stems not from harmonic or linear interruption, but from orchestral sonorities – Chrysothemis' strings suddenly fall silent, and an odd band of flutes, clarinets, bass clarinet and cor anglais replaces them for the space of Elektra's remark. At the same time, the motive played by the cor anglais (a), otherwise absent from the conversation, drops enigmatically into the musical discourse.

Elektra's obsessive A–D voice reappears at the opening of her confrontation with Klytämnestra, in her initial question to her mother (see Ex. 5). But now the musical disjunctions engendered by her remark are more serious. Klytämnestra's 'Ich habe keine guten Nächte' ('I have no peaceful nights') is supported by two alternating chords whose sonorous colour (B minor, half-diminished chord voiced F–A flat–C–D: bass pitches a tritone apart) is characteristically Klytämnestraesque; her query ends with a rising figure (a) which sends the cadential question off into other directions. Elektra's reply, three bars of pure D major, is a true harmonic, linear and metrical interruption, as well as an orchestral volte-face (in sudden muted trombones, muted trumpets, horn, oboe) in relation to Klytämnestra's harp and strings. More than this, where the absent-minded murmur to Chrysothemis was subsumed in surrounding E flat major, the question here resounds to a pivotal sonority (as the D major chord A–D–F sharp mutates in Elektra's fourth bar to B flat–D–F sharp) which deflects the B minor drone of Klytämnestra's opening towards B flat minor. Klytämnestra's response 'Wer älter wird' ('Whoever grows older'), on the point of the turn, lingers for an instant in resonances of Elektra's vocal sonority (the pitch D) and her instruments.

Chrysothemis' speech is a monologue to a deaf audience; Elektra does not reply except formulaically, and Chrysothemis' complaint must go on and on. This exchange is not an exchange at all, but rather another representation of solipsism, of Elektra walled in and indifferent. The confrontation between Elektra and Klytämnestra is another matter. Elektra, who wishes 'to speak with my mother, as never before', has a critical truth to reveal. Klytämnestra, who 'will not hear' the sibilant whispers of her confidantes, hangs upon Elektra's voice. In the conversation about the 'sacrificial victim', Klytämnestra probes every syllable for its meaning, even as Elektra asks her, 'Kannst du mich nicht erraten?' ('Can't you guess?').[20] The

Example 5

harmonic and linear choreographies project the two different exchanges. In Chrysothemis' speech, Elektra's remark – her obsessive A–D – is the merest ruffle in Chrysothemis' musical argument. In the exchange with Klytämnestra, the same Elektra-voice, no longer turned inward but thunderously phatic, is heard, interrupts, derails and redirects the passage.

Elektra's obsessed voice is woven into a third, more extended passage, the brief annunciation of Orestes' death which opens the opera's second half. A few remarks about the origins of the text may be in order. Hofmannsthal had eliminated the central (and lengthy) 'eyewitness' narrative in Sophocles' play, in which Orestes' Tutor tells in epic fashion of the Delphic chariot races, where Orestes 'struck the edge of a pillar and broke his axle in the centre; he himself was thrown from the rails of the chariot and tangled in the reins'. The Tutor's epic lie is so circumstantial, given so much temporal weight, that it seems almost to overbalance the play. Made uneasy by this enigmatically vast scale, many critics have read foreshadowings of Orestes' doom – torment at the Furies' hands, a fate not otherwise adumbrated in Sophocles – into the narrative's metaphors of dragging and enmeshment.

Hofmannsthal made Chrysothemis into the bearer of the tale, now a highly compressed narrative of what she has heard narrated: ironically, she becomes the very 'Bote von einem Boten von dem Bruder' ('messenger of a messenger from our brother') whose absence she had earlier regretted. The passage is possibly an experiment in imitating the repetitive language of hysterics, which Hofmannsthal knew from Freud's and Breuer's *Studien über Hysterie*. Freud wrote, in the case of 'Frau Emmy v. N.', of his patient's narrative being accompanied by 'multiple repetitions of her protective verbal formula (*Seien Sie still! – Reden Sie nichts! Rühren Sie mich nicht an!*)'.[21] The similarity to Elektra's *Schutzformel* 'Sei still!' (made with a gesture, as the stage directions indicate, 'to fend off [Chrysothemis], as if mad') may well be coincidental; nevertheless, the saturation of the annunciation scene with repeated formulae, for both speakers, is remarkably high, even in brief excerpts:

CHRYSOTHEMIS (*schreiend*) Orest! Orest ist tot!
ELEKTRA (*winkt ihr ab, wie von Sinnen*) Sei still!
CHRYSOTHEMIS (*dicht bei ihr*) Orest is tot!
(*Elektra bewegt die Lippen*)
CHRYSOTHEMIS Ich kam hinaus, da wussten sie's schon! Alle
standen herum und alle wussten's schon,
nur wir nicht.

ELEKTRA (*dumpf*) Niemand weiss es.
CHRYSOTHEMIS　　　　　　　　　　　　Alle wissen's!
ELEKTRA　　　　　Niemand kann's wissen: denn es ist nicht wahr.
(*Chrysothemis wirft sich verzweifelt auf den Boden*)
ELEKTRA (*Chrysothemis emporreissend*)
　　　　　　　Es ist nicht wahr! Es ist nicht wahr!
　　　　　　　Ich sag' dir doch, es ist nicht wahr!

CHRYSOTHEMIS (*screaming*) Orestes! Orestes is dead!
ELEKTRA (*makes a gesture to fend her off, as if mad*) Be quiet!
CHRYSOTHEMIS　　　Orestes is dead!
(*Elektra moves her lips*)
CHRYSOTHEMIS　　　I came out; they already knew it.
　　　　　　　They were all standing about, and they all
　　　　　　　knew it; only we did not know.
ELEKTRA (*in a hollow voice*) No one knows it.
CHRYSOTHEMIS　　　They all know it!
ELEKTRA　　　　　No one *can* know it, for it is not true.
(*Chrysothemis, in despair, throws herself to the ground*)
ELEKTRA (*dragging Chrysothemis up*) It is not true! It is not true, I tell you,
　　　　　　　it is not true!

Strauss made few changes in this iterative language; if anything, he emphasised it with further word repetitions.[22]

The musical realisation of the annunciation scene is worth considering in some detail. The scene might be viewed as a classic example of 'fluctuating tonality', in Schoenberg's sense,[23] since the framing key of E flat minor is continually challenged by musical impulses from the sphere of D minor (whose key signature is, in fact, in force throughout the scene). One has doubts, however, of Schoenberg's approbation for Strauss's brand of fluctuation; the two keys are often juxtaposed baldly and laterally, as Elektra's 'obsessive voice' with its characteristic pitches A and D interrupts in shouts of 'Es ist nicht wahr!' ('It's not true!'), often creating vertical sonorities that agglomerate triads from the two keys (see Ex. 8 below).

The opposition of the two keys may, however, be less important than the opposition of the two pitches E flat and F flat/E natural, often as vocal sonorities, yet heard initially in the orchestral flourish that opens the scene (see Ex. 6).[24] This clash is enmeshed within subsequent harmonic oscillations between E flat minor and D. Chrysothemis' vocal line in her first long speech circles around E flat as if tethered to the pitch (see Ex. 7). Chrysothemis holds to this E flat, first struck as a dissonant pitch over remnants of D minor/major; in the counterpoint between voice and orchestra (chiefly cor anglais, celli, horn, trumpet) the pitch sounds ceaselessly (when Chryso-

Example 6

themis turns from it, the instruments take it up). Insistence on this single pitch forces the harmonic fabric back to E flat minor (that is, it is not the 'dissonant note' E flat that is 'resolved', but the harmony that twists to affirm E flat as inescapable tonic).

Elektra's third, most forceful denial opposes to Chrysothemis' E flat drone a 'brighter' E natural (see Ex. 8). 'Es ist nicht wahr!': Elektra's obsessive A–D voice once more. But the statement (both musical and epistemological) is undermined by what follows, a 'polytonal' passage (a) which is an orchestral echo (in its agglomerated E flat minor and A major triads) of Chrysothemis' first 'ist tot', sung to the tritone E flat–A (b). Elektra's 'Es ist nicht wahr!', even as she repeats the words, slides from her E to Chrysothemis' E flat. She is drawn into a hopeless mimicry of Chrysothemis' sounds.

The release of tension we sense at the end of this passage, the final downward relaxation into C sharp minor, is appropriate to what follows, the narrative of the narrative. Chrysothemis can maintain a semblance of distance and control as long as she is merely the 'Bote von einem Boten von dem Bruder', a messenger describing messengers. Strauss made a brilliant stroke in gradually reintroducing the pitch E flat as Chrysothemis begins to leave this distancing frame, drawing near to the single line that remains of the true narrative. The final, sweeping E flat minor cadence (Fig. 22a) shadows the words that tell not of death's messengers, but of death itself, of Orestes dragged by his maddened horses, 'von seinen Pferden geschlagen, und geschleift'.

If Elektra's 'Armes Geschöpf!' is solipsistic, her 'Träumst du, Mutter?' a shard directed outwards that severs the harmonic web it touches, what are we to make of this third, far more complicated

Example 7

Example 8

stretch, which also resounds with Elektra's characteristic 'obsessive voice'? In the drama of hearing, this annunciation scene is a critical node, at which Elektra, at last compelled to listen, hears and believes what is untrue. And, having listened, she has begun to sing with Chrysothemis' despairing voice. In the collapse and loss of her own 'obsessed voice' (the passage in Ex. 8), she takes up, for the first time in the opera, music heard outside, music she has not created.

IV

Elektra creates music: we must return, in the end, to her epigram, 'The music comes from me'. As our own epigrammatic finale, we might speculate further on Strauss's means for creating this illusion, for ceding to Elektra the 'voice of the composition'.

For one thing, the music to which Elektra lays claim – the joyful music following Chrysothemis' 'Es ist der Bruder drin im Haus', the duet, the maenadic dance at the end – is derived broadly from her own monologue; the end of the opera may be seen as a final transformation of thematic material laid out in the monologue, such as the 'Orestes' rhapsody in A flat major, or the dithyrambic dance rhythms. Given the monologue's prophetic text – Elektra, after all, foresees the triumphal dance – this is in itself hardly surprising.

The point may, however, be amplified by considering the strong signals for formal song that are embedded in the monologue, which is thus not just a monologue, but in some sense a musical performance. What Cone called 'occasions for song' are unequivocal in most operatic works, and when Orfeo sings 'Che farò senza Euridice' before the gates of hell, he knows he is performing,[25] just as Manrico in his *Romanza* knows he sings (as does the tenor who begins 'Di rigori armato il seno' before a German-speaking princess). These 'occasions for song' are set apart from the normal discourse of opera, in which characters do not hear their own voices, do not hear the music that is their means of expression. But by the latter part of the nineteenth century the situation is no longer so clear. In this, Wagner must be regarded as a central influence: what is the Rome Narrative in *Tannhäuser* – beginning as performed song and slipping midway into another mode – if not the boundary between heard and unheard music, dissolved at last?

In Elektra's monologue, Hofmannsthal made his own version of the epicedia and 'sorrowful laments' that Sophocles' Elektra names as her only remaining form of speech. Threnody, dirge, lament,

epicedium: these are musical forms. Mourning is formal, intensified
by the hieratic effect of music. Goethe knew well the effect; many of
the songs embedded in his plays, like the 'Song of the Fates' in
Iphigenie auf Tauris (a text set by Brahms), represent moments of
great solemnity.

Traces of epicedium and lament pass into Strauss's monologue for
Elektra not only in touches of affective colour (minor key, slow
tempo) but also in the effect of a song, in the way Strauss frames the
opening. Elektra's 'Allein! weh, ganz allein' is calculated as an echo
of recitative (startling in this aggressively anti-conventional opera), a
rhythmically diffuse, introductory flourish before the grave spondaic
thump (V–I) that signals the song's formal beginning. This is not
mere soliloquy (aria), but something Elektra has sung, every night,
at her appointed hour. We should perhaps not extend the argument
overmuch; yet if this is Elektra's song, *she* has created its music: such
is the illusion of 'occasions for song'.

The music to which she sings her epigram makes the point in
another way (see Ex. 9). This is no more than a contrapuntal elabora-

Example 9

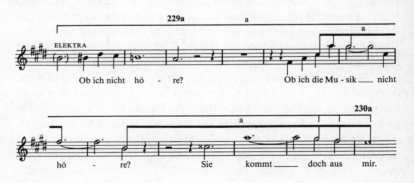

tion, on two levels, of the four-note motive that opens the annunciation scene (cf. Ex. 6). The figure, most emphatically, does not belong
to Elektra's voice, but rather is something Chrysothemis compels her
to hear, when she breaks the news of Orestes' death. But Elektra,
having heard the figure long ago, here takes it as her own, transforms
it into melody, into a musical phrase of great beauty; in transforming
it, what is she but a composer, teasing substance out of a dormant
and common seed?

The protean Elektra of this reading is a far cry from the empty vessel, the woman without access to deed or action, envisaged by some critics (those, it must be said, who are deaf to the opera's voices, reading words alone). In this respect, *Elektra* belongs to a group of twentieth-century operas – such as *Lulu* – in which the considerable interest of the feminine roles owes little to nineteenth-century operatic tradition. It might seem odd that Strauss, cynical, paternalistic and hardly a feminist advocate, would so efface himself, cede so much of his narrating voice, in a way Wagner (for one) seldom countenanced. As Joseph Kerman has suggested in another context, the character may have overwhelmed its actual creator and carried him to a peculiar transcendence he did not otherwise achieve.[26]

But while few would deny that *Elektra* has a power not elsewhere duplicated in Strauss's œuvre, it is harder to focus upon the reasons. The conventional explanations – the violence of the subject, the literate poetic text, the sheer din of the orchestra, the daring of nascent atonality, the musical 'structure', the genial *Effektmalerei* – all seem incomplete. Many of Strauss's operatic works possess these same qualities (albeit in varying degrees, and with variously happy results). What sets *Elektra* apart is, perhaps, our sense of another power, the 'polyphony beyond counterpoint' of the voice that shadows the text, the voice of the music, the narrator's semiotic voice, the vocal personae. Above all, *Elektra* is a clamour of tongues, and Elektra's voice, among many, sings in animated, sonorous congress.

8 The orchestration of 'Elektra': a critical interpretation

ROBIN HOLLOWAY

I

The problem in considering the orchestration of *Elektra* is to recon-
cile Strauss's instruction to play the work 'as if [it] were by Mendelssohn: fairy music'[1] with the largest forces required by any opera
in the repertory. Its starting-point is the orchestra as constituted for
the *Ring*, but the aesthetic goal is very different. Wagner deploys his
vast forces to produce homogeneity, roundedness and warmth; contrasts of colour and weight are gradual, as befits his scale and speed,
and even when the sonority is at its most extreme (*Götterdämmerung*
Act II) there remains a fullness that is always built up from a powerful bass. Strauss's use of the same forces plus some extras comes
after *Salome* and all but one of the symphonic poems whose tendency
has been to break up the homogeneity, splash on the colour, raise the
tessitura and take brilliance of detail to the very edge of virtuosity.
He can be more brutalistic and more brilliant, heavier and lighter, all
with an electricity and a rapidity of change that would be out of
place even in the more extravagant reaches of *Parsifal* where the
sources of *Elektra* mainly lie.

Brass is exactly as in the *Ring*: eight horns, of which four double
two pairs of Wagner tubas whose bass is the contrabass tuba; three
trombones and a contrabass; for normal purposes three trumpets
and a bass trumpet, strengthened in the heftiest climaxes by three
extra players (and thus overtopping Wagner's demands). The woodwinds are basically in fours: piccolo and three flutes (1 also doubling
piccolo); three oboes (3 doubling cor anglais) and heckelphone;
three bassoons and contrabassoon. Strauss alas did not follow up the
somewhat gingerly experiment with a saxophone choir in the *Symphonia Domestica*, but clarinets are expanded with typical turn-of-
the-century generosity to eight in all: four ordinary clarinets (B flat
and A); one small in E flat, one bass (B flat); and a hapless couple of

128

basset horns strayed out of their native eighteenth century. Here, then, there is a far wider spectrum of timbre than in Wagner (as well as four more players). But the more specifically colouristic aspects of *Elektra* are modest by some contemporary standards (*Rapsodie espagnole*, *Firebird*, Mahler 8, *Gurrelieder*): though the two harps may be doubled from p. 353[2] to the end, the celeste is optional. Two timpani players are required, and the percussion is straightforward; the list at the start of the score omits the *two* pairs of castanets that clack four times on p. 11 and the switch (*Rute*) that spurs Klytämnestra's procession into motion on pp. 75–91 ('a confused noise of trampling beasts, of whips, of muffled screams . . .').[3] The latter had first been heard on p. 23 when the young servant-girl was beaten.

More seriously incomplete, or at least ambiguous, is this list's breakdown of the strings. Violins are divided into firsts, seconds and thirds, eight in each, making 24 in all, eight less than the 32 in the standard *de luxe* turn-of-the-century division of 16 firsts and 16 seconds. Do the missing eight help swell the violas up to the eighteen mentioned on the first page of music (as opposed to the list, which only requires *six*)? No, because almost from the start and unmistakably by pp. 20–1 all three viola parts (6+6+6) are well below violin range. (Strauss is notoriously cavalier about notes off the bottom of the violins, though in *Elektra* he gives all 24 just six crotchets' rest to retune the G-string down to encompass the three low F semiquavers on p. 26.) In fact it is the other way about: the top third of the eighteen violas has twice to become fourth violins, for the recognition scene and Elektra's Hymn before Action (pp. 272–98) and from p. 342 to the end (Elektra's apotheosis and death). The score says 'muta in IV. Violinen'; whether this is a change of *function* for players who still remain playing their violas, or involves a change of actual *instrument*, is not made clear. But the result is in effect the standard firsts/seconds division of the violins. The twelve cellos are divided into firsts and seconds almost throughout, and there are eight double basses. (For comparison, the *Ring* asks for 16:16:12:12:8.) The 'house feature' of *Elektra*, strings laid out in nine parts – Vl. I, II, III; Vle I, II, III; Vcl. I, II; Cb. – is more frequent throughout the work than any standard layout.

With an orchestra of 20 woodwinds, 20 brass, heavy battery and 62 strings, 'fairy music' would seem to be an unobtainable goal. Whereas one's instinctive sense-impression of *Salome* is shimmer and spice (albeit quite thickly laid on), *Elektra* reverberates in the mind with its weight; its animal bloodiness; its screams, tearings, axings; its nightmares and processions; above all, the galumphing and colossal dance-motions with which it ends. The paradox can be evaded: perhaps it is just one of Strauss's notorious 'shrugs' – 'don't bother *me*; *I* don't know' – designed half-embarrassedly, half-teasingly to put questioners off the trail and escape culpability for his own excess. Or it can be circumvented by an exceptional performance, such as the *Elektra* under Carlos Kleiber that I saw at Covent Garden in 1977, where finesse and hairsplitting detail produced something quite different from the usual all-stops-out blow to the solar plexus. Or it can be laboriously explored by the commentator to yield what fruit it may.

What Carlos Kleiber missed was the normative in the work, the straight tutti usage which provides a gauge by which to measure its extremes. Its most and its least inspired sections are equally atypical of the special internal balance whereby hyperstrain becomes the norm. Least inspired by common consent is the long outburst for the 'normal' sister Chrysothemis (Figs. 75–114) and its varied return much later when Elektra plays upon this very normalcy to get Chrysothemis to act with her after the false news of Orestes' death (Figs. 52a–82a).[4] Though in *Elektra* these passages jar, in the context of Strauss as a whole they are typical enough – the Strauss who produces music 'as a cow gives milk', all the way from the genial banalities of his teens to the wind-band Sonatinas of the 1940s. The orchestra is so classically used that we forget its hugeness – that, for instance, all eight horns are in play from Fig. 102 till just after 112. It is like a turn-of-the-century solution to the problems of balance when the post-Wagnerian orchestra plays Beethoven: simply double (or even quadruple) all winds. Since the 'house feature' of the nine-part string texture is also retained, the result is a golden churn of Happy Workshop ease, as undistinguished in substance as it is masterly in its layout for maximum warmth and flow.

The recognition scene (Figs. 148a–55a) is also characterised by this golden strings-and-horns sound. The strings are given melody and flowing accompaniment figures; the halo of divisi and solo players does not conceal the basic layout as Vl. I and II, Vle, Vcl. I and II, Cb., simplifying by Fig. 153a into only three parts. A few woodwinds are sparingly used to double and intensify; all eight horns provide a glowing core of organ harmony, at its most ardent at Fig. 154a where the paragraph's point of climax simultaneously begins to droop. The whole scene sounds like the work of a Mantovani of genius.

Utterly gorgeous in sonority, it yet remains what Busoni would call 'transcribed'.

So the centre of Strauss's orchestra in *Elektra*, in its supreme passage and in its two dullest and most dutiful stretches, is the combination of horns and strings. In *Elektra* an abnorm in its very normalness, this kind of sound relates to the basis of Strauss's orchestration throughout his life. I want to stay with strings and horns separately for a moment before moving on to the less absolutely quintessential instruments. Even here, at the heart of his orchestra, there are usages that are typical and usages that are special: usages and abusages of the heart.

Pretty normative is the passage from Fig. 18a: here the strings in four parts (all Vl.; Vle; all Vcl.; Cb.) would *look* like an advanced turn-of-the-century string quartet (as it might be Schoenberg Op. 7 or Zemlinsky No. 2) – four busy independent thematic lines (the bass with long sustained notes as well) – were it not for the wind and brass doubling the lines, the usual horn–organ-part (anything from one to eight) and the more massive wind harmony towards the climax at Fig. 22a. More straightforward still is the first appearance of the Orestes-recognition theme, in its native A flat (from bar 9 of Fig. 45): all violins unison, all cellos an octave below, harmony on violas à3 and double basses à2, doubled by light low woodwinds and horns; horn 1 also doubles the tune in the lower (cello) octave; and the poignant A flat minor phrase at its end is joined by a solo oboe in the upper (violin) octave.

From such instances of strings-as-foundation-of-the-orchestra I move to places where they are anything but. At Fig. 47 (through to 50) the violins split into their three, first joining with the three-part violas for skirls and banks of parallel chords in three, four and six parts, then doubled by low woodwinds, with four horns, also in parallel, pulling away in contrary motion, as also, well below, the basses, contrabassoon and contrabass tuba. Pure eye-and-ear onomatopoeia in the eight-part whirl for strings that for six bars at Fig. 233a drenches the ongoing beat of Elektra's final dance in 'the ocean, the twenty-fold vaster ocean' which in the very moment of revenge keeps her from rejoicing. More complex, the string textures at Figs. 135–8, where the banks of unrelated triads spaced thus – Vl. III + Vle I + Vcl. I (a); Vle II + Vcl. I (b); Vle III + Vcl. II; all three lines doubled by three muted horns – are set against soft but penetrating chords on six solo violas. Such description makes heavy weather of an extraordinary effect which could not have been achieved more simply.

So to usage and abusage of the heart's other half: the eight horn players, including the four Wagner tubas taken up, after the fashion of the *Ring*, by the second quartet of hornists. Their norm, as we have seen, is a warm mass of organ-harmony. There are of course solo passages, but almost nothing of that highly individuated writing for the whole section which makes some of Strauss's later scores (above all *Capriccio*) look like the Schumann *Konzertstück* (a brief, partial exception comes in the six bars centring on Fig. 143a). *Elektra* is also the classic place for 'dreadful horn-writing' – un-idiomatic if exciting whoops and runs (for example, Fig. 188 to one after 196; Figs. 1a–4a), signalling the horn-player's son in his furthest revolt against nature.

The previous history of the Wagner tubas, in the *Ring* and Bruckner's last three symphonies, is one of exalted sublimity with elements of the bucolic (and a touch of the grotesque for Fafner). Their sublimity is used early in the scene between Elektra and the stranger before he is recognised as her brother (Figs. 123a–6a). Though the four trombones join them (on p. 250 the names of contrabass tuba and contrabass trombone are mistakenly reversed in the score), the timbre is tuba-ish in the most normative way, and all five of the family retain this low-horn organ-harmony foundation in the superb fourteen-bar sentence beginning at Fig. 126a. As against this, well within the intention for which Wagner invented the instruments, there is writing that pushes them to an extreme. Their first significant entry (Figs. 48–51) had been unobtrusive; from Fig. 123 they are warming up (à la Elgar); from 127, the start of Klytämnestra's entry procession, they begin to be fully characterised, with the big yawps ('heraufschleifen') sticking out like an animal in pain; and from just after 130 the bullocky sound of their unison is a powerful ingredient in the general mêlée (their part coming in to 132 actually *looks* like Fafner's motive). The first part of the Klytämnestra scene (Fig. 135 to fourth bar of 141) extends this new character and colour for these big noble horns, a kind of hormone-charged alto–tenor throb, suggestive of her sexuality, her guilty bed redolent with memories and nightmares, her diseases of body and mind. (It seems a bit silly that three of them have to change back for only *one chord* at Fig. 145 before resuming their tubas just after 152.) Nothing else the Wagner tubas play is so striking as here, though this new colour and character are indispensable to the music beginning at Fig. 177, when Klytämnestra describes her bad nights, right through to the end of the scene and Elektra's premature triumph (Fig. 260); and thence into the orchestral interlude reversing that triumph, which will be considered later.

II

Strings, horns and Wagner tubas are the melody, base and core of the *Elektra* orchestra. The mass of the woodwinds, even the heavier or more brilliant brass, are extra to this basic sound, and their parts are more a matter of notable individual moments and, sometimes, extended stretches than ongoing background with an occasional sense of patient routine. I should like now to consider Strauss's orchestra as a tutti; again the idea of 'normal' and 'abnormal' can be useful, recognising always that, within the claustrophobia of this work, the two tend to be reversed.

Three interconnected examples will show the *Elektra*-tutti at its most usual. First, the end of Elektra's monologue, with its foretaste of the triumphal dance that will succeed righteous revenge. This passage (Fig. 53 to just after 64), the most sustained continuity in the work so far, is in musical substance as in orchestration a magnificent blow-up of the Johann Strauss waltz, with singing strings and emphatic rhythm-marking harmony on the brass, the whole sound underpinned by a 'continuo' of two timp-players, triangle, cymbals, bass drum (though not the ubiquitous side drum of the Viennese dance-bands) and two harps (always in unison). Particularly successful as the dance gets under way is the combination of dry pounding dance-rhythm with sostenuto melody. From five after Fig. 58 the recognition theme in $\frac{3}{2}$ is placed across the dance in $\frac{6}{4}$ whose principal figure (♩. ♪ ♩) is at Fig. 59 bounced with heavy lightness across the entire orchestra, while the melody is passed among the upper strings (with unobtrusive woodwind doublings); the holes in this aerated texture are imperceptibly plugged by soft sostenuto whole-bar chords on (mainly) trumpets and trombones. The totality, made up of layer upon layer each incomplete in itself, leaves space for the harps' arpeggii to come through, subsidiary though they be, together with the delicious little flourish on two flutes in the third bar of Fig. 59. All this by way of contrast with the onslaught of the tutti from four before Fig. 62 to its fade around 64 as Chrysothemis appears.

The passage from the seventh bar of Fig. 172a to the sixth of 180a, when, at the end of the recognition scene, Elektra hymns the deed that is now about to be done, takes up and extends the lyric strain of the first waltz-dream. The texture is now open, singing, surging, basically on strings. The previous $^6_4$ galumphing is replaced by the organ-like sostenuto chords, on all five tubas, that characterise Orestes; the percussion (all present except triangle) is used in occasional strokes and tingles rather than for rhythmic underlining – which is transferred to the tattoo-motives derived from the Agamemnon theme (𝅘𝅥𝅯𝅘𝅥𝅯 𝅘𝅥 𝄾), crackling across the texture in $^4_4$ on aggressive brass (trombones, trumpets) but very soft. The mastery of Strauss's fluency in getting up heat, exaltation and shine on pretty indifferent musical materials can ride even the appalling eight bars at Fig. 177a, when the recognition theme is smeared across the texture by the first four horns in unison – a moment as crude as the comparable Figs. 58–60 was subtle.

The second dance-episode, from Fig. 236a to just after 260a, completes this strain in the work, taking up both its singing and its strenuous aspects into a kind of dance-'Liebestod', a hymn of ritualised motion more psychological than physical. Its first stages (after the initial racket of arriving at C major dies down) are entirely lyrical, with singing strings and surging inner parts derived from the passage just discussed, and its sostenuto harmony now on the eight horns and the four trombones alternately. The festive percussion gradually joins, this time including a glockenspiel (after Fig. 244a) – and from this point the Agamemnon-tattoo is transformed into a hoofy downbeat from which each bar, then each half-bar, is launched of the powerful dance-motion at Fig. 247a. Two bars after Fig. 248a this turns into the ♩ 𝄾 ♪♩ motive, not at once obliterating the cantabile but predominating more and more till from around 252a [see Plate 5] it sweeps all before it to the four climactic bars at 254a. Thereafter it retreats to the bass (the double basses are actually marked *leicht*), and by Fig. 257a is only kept up on the two harps and triangle (the clarinets doubling the harps do not count, since this motive when played *legato* loses its character), while soprano and orchestra sing with *Arabella*-like lyricism. From the seventh bar of Fig. 258a it grows suddenly and gigantically; seven bars suffice to achieve maximum volume (all eight horns, all seven trumpets and a proper cymbal-crash) at 260a.

These three episodes taken together make a 'Dance of the *Überweib*'-cum-'Liebestod' whose athletic aspect evidently grows from the 'Ride of the Valkyries' and whose lyric aspect, less evidently but demonstrably, derives from the flowing $^6_4$ of Mendelssohn's *Schöne Melusine* and her warmer-blooded descendants the Rhinemaidens

5: A page from Strauss's autograph score of *Elektra* (from Fig. 253a/3 to Fig. 254a/4 of the published score)

(see the eleven bars from the key-change just after Fig. 255a – the timps in particular are straight out of the first scene of *Das Rheingold*, the musical substance out of the Mendelssohn). The whole is swathed in a vastly exploded Viennese waltz, updated to the Palm Court of the Ritz Hotel *c*. 1908. It is a tribute to Strauss's panache that he can carry off such a *mélange* with complete lack of self-consciousness: confronted with such triumphalism, 'tis folly to be wise!

By contrast with such gigantism, what Strauss might mean by 'fairy music' begins to become a little clearer. Two outstanding passages come to mind; though neither is exactly gossamer-like, they both have a speed and fluency that derive ultimately from Mendelssohn's scherzo-types. The fleet § of the interlude, from five before Fig. 261 to the work's halfway break before 1a, is the first really fast music in the opera; its sharpness and apparent gaiety render at once the unholy exhilaration of Klytämnestra's joy at the news of Orestes' death and the lighting of torches to banish the nightmares she has just divulged. The starting-point is the scherzo from *A Midsummer Night's Dream*, given weight, grandeur and length by Loge's big set-piece in Nibelheim, then restored by Strauss to the original quicksilver movement while retaining something of the Wagnerian weight (the ♩ ♪ ♩ ♪ figure on seven low clarinets and cor anglais, and then on the four Wagner tubas, even on the first page). The virtuosity has been learnt from his own *Till* and the ¹²⁄₈ section of *Zarathustra*: the scales and arpeggii on woodwinds and strings (always at least doubled – he is not so reckless now as earlier – and more conveniently disposed for the instruments).[5] The passage is not lightly scored – the result is more tumultuous than delicate – but the writing is both foolproof and absolutely transparent.

The second Mendelssohn scherzo-type – the ²⁄₄ scurry – comes when, abandoned by her sister, Elektra goes it alone, scrabbling dementedly for the axe and watched towards the end by a silent, unrecognised and unrecognising brother (Figs. 110a–123a). The lower strings scurry around in staccato semiquavers, articulated with gruppetti on low slithy woodwinds (basset horns, bass clarinet, bassoons single and double); the texture works rapidly up to yelps for the upper strings and woodwind, and the Agamemnon triplet theme pierces through on four muted trumpets and side drum; as all this sinks back to earth, Agamemnon's repeated-note theme rises up to die on one soft, high, muted trumpet-note. Motion starts up again at Fig. 114a; at a second lull, the theme that spells out Agamemnon's name is heard on lugubrious oboe and bassoon in octaves, weirdly spaced between the high violin repeated semiquavers and the single-note interrogation, held now on two muted trumpets. For the third resumption of motion at Fig. 116a, both top and bottom of the texture retain the semiquavers, gradually coming down to meet in the middle occupied at first only by occasional spasmodic jerks on solo horns. From Fig. 118a sustained heavy brass begin very softly to fill out the bass registers as Orestes appears; they make a sudden lunge into Fig. 120a as Elektra perceives the stranger who watches her frenzied activity. As she questions him and bids him move on, the little scherzando episode gutters out into the Wagner-tuba chords that begin the recognition scene (Fig. 123a). Behind all this is, surely, another, very distant, fairy-Mendelssohnian source: the centre of the *Midsummer Night's Dream* Overture, where 'things go bump in the night' – sudden holes in the texture, alien blasts on horns or ophicleide, but distant and muffled, the delicate perpetual motion constantly set off-course, only to resume again in another place. This distant source, greatly strengthened and muddied by its recreation in the first scene of *Das Rheingold* when Alberich scrambles to reach the treasure (grotesque wind gruppetti and flailing lower strings) is recreated by Strauss with a repossession of the Mendelssohnian transparency and speed to depict the thoughts as well as the motion of the demented soil-scrabbler; the next, surprising, stop on this line, the ultimate in this kind of animated freeze of suspense, is the 'Danse de la Terre' from *The Rite of Spring*.

From these two 'fairy tuttis' it is possible to extend the scope of the word to cover something rather different: the music, in which *Elektra* abounds, of split hairs, screaming nerves, nightmare hallucinations, visceral obsessions of blood and shame. The paradox *here* is, rather, that Strauss the easy-going, none-too-thin-skinned 'good chap' is such a master of these discomforts, rendering them with the physical immediacy of a nettle-sting or a mosquito at your ear. Or perhaps only someone so at ease in his own skin could do such things at all, with the sort of externalised brilliance of a master-mimic or hal-lucinator. Questions like this, where the orchestration seems to point straight to the composer's innermost qualities and failings, will be taken up at the end of this essay.

Meanwhile, *black* fairy-music: nightmares, curses, enthralments, obsessions, horrors. Fig. 64: as Elektra's first waltz-dream fades on to a single *pianissimo* woodwind octave (first harp and triangle all that's left of the percussion 'continuo'), Chrysothemis timidly utters her sister's name, snatching her from her reverie (one quaver 'sehr stark' on thirteen brass instruments and timps with wooden stick) and bringing forth words of wounding contempt. The texture is instantaneously turned into a thing of horror. High F minor is sustained on three solo violins doubling a flute and two piccolos, simultaneous with four muted horns on B minor. As the first harp tremolandos on the F minor, a pungent bank of two low oboes, cor anglais and heckelphone, supported by bassoons, basset horns and solo unmuted violas and cellos, swells up from the B minor triad in a distorted fragment of the preceding dance music. An abrupt Agamemnon-gesture across a wide-spaced B minor for the tutti muted strings is overlapped by three trumpets and one trombone, all muted, entering on the low B minor; their crescendo, obliterating the slide of the three solo violins to a C major triad, precipitates a new spasm of the distorted dance, now pitched around a low F minor triad, and set sharply off by the tutti string pizzicato as well as the four muted brass. One soft chord underlies Chrysothemis' words ('Ist mein Gesicht dir so verhasst?') – the dominant seventh on B flat, hinting at the E flat of her big outburst beginning a few pages later at Fig. 75, and warmly scored on two bassoons and two *un*muted horns. During this the solo strings quickly mute and the whole body, with that choked quality of muted strings played with violence, gives the heavily-accented chords that break up Elektra's harsh reply: in between the two last, well under her unsupported voice, the Agamemnon theme in octaves on two clarinets and bass clarinet (helped at first by basset horns) begins hollow and soft, swelling to a reedy *fortissimo.*

After such punctilious exactness in orchestral layout as this, the passages of flesh-creeping sound-effects that follow can seem, arguably, a little cheap. Elektra's laugh at Fig. 71, and the diverging streams of parallel diminished fifths, weirdly spaced, that evoke 'the strangled breath, the death-rattle of murdered ones' in the palace's unhallowed walls (though the spacing at Fig. 73 – two flutes, bass clarinet, contrabassoon – anticipates late Janáček, Birtwistle, Colin Matthews), are on the edge; over it, the moment at Fig. 89 when 'storms shake the hut' and Strauss feels obliged to break the golden flow of Chrysothemis with five bars of bad onomatopoeia. Another dubious place is the passage beginning eighth bar of Fig. 114; yet within a few seconds of these routine scarifications, we have the four bars at 119 which in their naked exactitude of imaginative detail (the passage for four bassoons; the fourth on the timps and the third on low trombones; the semiquaver run up a B flat clarinet, the E flat, the piccolo; the trumpet solo so unusual in contour) are worthy of the *Survivor from Warsaw* which they acutely resemble.

Around Fig. 157 comes the basset horn's moment of glory, recalling this time the fantastical decorative Schoenberg of *Pierrot* or the *Serenade* Op. 24, and followed at Fig. 158 by arabesques on a solo violin straight out of Kundry's seduction of Parsifal; at 159 the brass attack produces a remarkable effect, simultaneous *sforzandi* on one horn and one trombone, and *piano* on the second players (all four muted). The grotesquely high pizzicati on violins II/III here, doubled by piccolo and E flat clarinet, seem to have been recalled from the second movement of Mahler's Fourth Symphony. Going further into Klytämnestra's scene, the pages from just before Fig. 170 are particularly rich in such detailed instrumental inventiveness. The dispersal here of the dark *Tristan/Wozzeck* poison into *Parsifal/Arabella* healing is quite brilliant. The twelve or so bars from Fig. 175 are extraordinary: the seven clarinets (including basset horns and bass) lurch in almost *Wein*-ian drunkenness, against light staccato repeated notes ascending chromatically on flute and piccolo in octaves, and the whirring triplets, creepily legato, of a solo violin and solo viola; the whole over deep sustained contrabass trombone notes disappearing into the low brass B minor as mother and daughter are left alone together at Fig. 177.

We have reached this chord once before, in talking of Klytämnestra's bullocky Wagner tubas. They are muted, and the top note of the four-note chord is doubled by two muted horns, the other three by three muted trombones, the whole underpinned by the muted bass tuba. Above this, Klytämnestra's bad nights unfold in dully-bright chords on string pizzicati double and triple stops, the two harps, a glockenspiel catching the top part, and one flute 'spreading' the chord with the plucked sound, a very successful idea. The contrast just before Klytämnestra's first words of clear soft woodwind F minor and low dim plucked B minor is equally telling, as also the succession of tiny obbligati accompaniments (bass clarinet, oboe and first horn, over four trombones and timpani) that accompany Elektra's first words, 'Träumst du, Mutter?' ('Do you dream, mother?'). The wind chording over deep trombones *ppp* doubled by harps *forte* at Fig. 180, the contrabassoon's moment of glory at 181 – this is writing of classic simplicity, without a hint of the cheap effects which come so easily to Strauss the orchestrator or Strauss the composer: best is the barest moment of all, the solo trumpet (now *not* muted, which is its genius) tattooing softly on low D, doubled by harp, an octave below Klytämnestra's sudden long-held D on 'eine *Kraft*' (the *power* that lies within each one of her amulets). At Fig. 186 there is another brilliant adaptation of Wagner, when the two lower Wagner tubas, doubled at the unison by contrabass tuba and at the lower octave by contrabassoon, for eighteen bars convert Fafner the mighty monster into some appalling tapeworm, spiral bacillus or horror of the imagination. The timbre of the orchestral tutti from Fig. 188 onwards is astonishing in its evocation of choking claustrophobia – the four muted horns (doubled by muted celli in four parts) running a band of parallel close harmony, in the strangulated top of their register, against a similar band of the three violin groups and first violas (doubled by three flutes and the first clarinet), emptying out into great steam-choked chords around Fig. 192, where high trumpets *pianissimo* interlock with flutes and piccolo.[6]

It would be possible to continue at this level of detail for the rest of this extraordinary scene. Just one more example will suffice, the wonderful use of the cymbal to reintroduce Elektra's festive dance music, stealing over her as she engineers her mother's incipient collapse (Fig. 205). Much more effectively does this simple stroke suggest her 'secret smile' than did the elaborate onomatopoeia of her laughter (Fig. 71); the powerful pull of the returning dance-jubilation in the pages following is all the stronger for their restraint, culminating in the magical arrival at a *ppp* C major at Fig. 212 (which will return all-stops-out at 236a), with soft cymbals and triangle, and ♩. ♪♩ just touched in by the brass.[7]

No accident that the most part of such details come in the work's first half: *chez* Strauss there is always a sense of routine later on, even in a work like this, which depends upon maximum intensity. Once he has found his habits, he does not tax them overmuch, lets things go with their own momentum, then pulls himself together for the final stretch. It had been so with *Salome* and was to persist, through *Der Rosenkavalier*, *Intermezzo* and *Arabella*, right up to *Capriccio*, irrespective of style or subject-matter.

III

It is interesting to return, via a passage like Figs. 188–93, to reconsider the orchestra of *Elektra* not as a tutti but rather as a corporate multiplicity of such details as I have described. Strauss is not by instinct a 'chamber'-orchestrator like Mahler and Schoenberg; as with Wagner his is always a tutti conception. His erosion into detail is the result equally of his lively response to dangerous subjects and of the spirit of the age which saw in the large orchestra both an organism evolving ever-upwards and a machine capable of ever more complex precision. I want therefore before concluding to look at a few further tutti passages which show why he still remains the principal master of a particular epoch and manner of composing.

First the passage from Fig. 32 that takes us from the young servant girl's whipping to Elektra's first entry, with its brilliantly clear delineation of a V–I cadence in D harshed and excruciated by F minor. The whip is represented by the *Rute* (switch) doubling sharp F minor attacks on two oboes and high violas. Against this a three-note ostinato on four trumpets alternating the triads of F minor and F sharp minor is twice heard (♪ ♫ ⁷ ♪ | ♫); the instant it stops (second crotchet of second bar of Fig. 32) there is one more stroke of the whip (high celli and three bassoons); on the next quaver comes the entry, up high, of the sinuous theme, made out of Agamemnon, foreshadowing Elektra (loud, penetrating, but not harsh – all violins, plus two flutes, a clarinet in E flat and one in A); on the bar's fourth crotchet F minor enters powerfully on four muted trombones (discreetly helped by two low clarinets and the basset horns) underpinned by a low D on bass clarinet and four bassoons (including the contra, at the same octave); on the eighth quaver the four trumpets begin their ostinato again, overlapped this time at a quaver's distance by the timp on the A flat lower than that in the trombones' F minor, and at the next quaver by cellos and basses (unison, not an octave apart) with their same three-note rhythm emphasising the low D. All this is reproduced in the next three bars, but less loud and an octave lower, with modifications as required by the change of tessitura (the whipping is now on violas and cellos doubled by cor anglais and heckelphone, the trumpets' figure goes onto four horns and bass trumpet, the sinuous melody onto violas doubled by first oboe and two B flat clarinets). The next four bars see a drastic simplification of this hectic activity, simply alternating sundry blows in F minor with woodwind writhes and grimaces in D major, all over the lowest D in the orchestra, until the full presentation of the sinuous theme in D minor cadencing at Fig. 34.

The next of these passages, the entry of Klytämnestra's procession (Figs. 126–32), has already been noted for its use of the Wagner tubas. Indeed the quality and sonority of the orchestra as a whole is bullocky: the main motive itself, obstinately set across itself, stylises

the groan of the beast of burden (♩♪♪ ♩♪♪ / ♩ ♪ ♪ ♪ etc.), and
the placing, low but loud on all the strings, *muted*, colours the whole
texture with a veil of powerfully thwarted energy. From Fig. 129
bright but equally strangulated sounds cut through (a figure on flutes
and piccolo, oboes and cor anglais, and four muted trumpets), and
the strings demute over the next seven bars to present the diminution
of the main motive with maximum tone. From 130 the orchestra
starts to heave; the trombones (hitherto growling at the bottom)
begin to surge up in triplets, the bass woodwinds in semiquavers;
by 131 the entire orchestra is abandoned to a sea of scales in contrary
motion, across the bullock-groan high and low; and in the final three
bars all this is rent asunder by three eruptions of Agamemnon
triplets from the bottom to the top of the heaviest and most cutting
brass. The prototype is evidently the piling-up of the Nibelheim
treasure in Scene 4 of *Das Rheingold*; characteristically, Wagner
depicts from within, making an unforgettable spiritual image of
oppression, bondage, tyranny, while Strauss brilliantly depicts the
externals – the cracking whips, the groans, the sweat, the weight. The
final stages of the procession resemble a crazed version of Fricka's
entry in Act II of *Die Walküre*, but with Wotan's consort replaced
by Kundry. (Incidentally, while we're onto this kind of thing, the
closeness to Wagner's fate motive at Fig. 135 (see Chapter 6, Ex. 9f),
as the haunted queen cries out to the gods against her daughter's
presence lying so heavily upon her, must surely be deliberate.)

From these oppressive places to the exaltation of the recognition
scene; in particular Figs. 128a–30a. This, arguably the greatest
passage in the work, shows Strauss's powers of lyric paragraph-
building at their height. Its orchestration consists (as Piston would
say)[8] of three 'elements'. The first is the ♩. ♩ ♩. ♩ figure that persists throughout. In the first four bars (beginning at the second of
Fig. 128a) it is in octaves, on the upper the tutti violas and the cor
anglais, on the lower the tutti violins and a bassoon; a pair of
clarinets binds the two octaves by playing both. From the fifth bar
the upper octave goes to two flutes and an oboe, with solo violin, the
lower to the first basset horn with solo viola, the pair of clarinets
coming in and out, showing, in these five bars where the figure has
become a motion rather than a theme, their division, according to
the phrasing of the voice part and its harmony, into $2 \times 2\frac{1}{2}$. After
Fig. 129a the second woodwind players alternate on the figure (now
melodic again) with the first, and the tutti violins and violas with the

solo players, making these three bars into $2 \times 1\frac{1}{2}$. The heckelphone reinforces the lower octave, and a solo cello detaches itself from the internal melody to join the other two solo strings for the closing four bars of the phrase (the four into Fig. 130a), where the line is now in unison (parallel with, when not actually duplicating, the soprano) on these three, plus all three flutes, first oboe and first basset horn.

The internal melody also is doubled at the octave, on a pair of horns and tutti cellos divided à2; the lower octave is further reinforced by the bass clarinet. This full but potentially stolid sound is marvellously brought to life by being doubled throughout by both harps, a simple idea with unsimple results. When from the sixth bar of Fig. 128a the phrases become antiphonal, the answers are given to the second pair of horns, muted, and two bassoons, the cellos leaving only one solo player on the top octave, and the harps playing (at this same octave) in harmonics. The dialogue lasts for the five bars before Fig. 129a, when all the instruments that have been involved on the part (but omitting the pair of muted horns and the solo cello) and some that are new to it (the heckelphone, the second basset horn, the double basses) join to play what proves to be its final bar before coalescing into the passage's harmony.

The harmony has been spaced with economy and simplicity. In the initial four bars D minor is given in semibreves on lowish flutes and oboes, and two clarinets and two basset horns in their dullest register, brought to life by two soft high trombones doubled by two solo violas (who renew their sound every other bar, thus binding the chords together). There is a soft drum-stroke D on each first beat. When the harmony moves and the phrasing becomes more complex, the drum is silenced, the chords are sustained only by four woodwinds (flute 3, cor anglais, heckelphone, second basset horn) and the bass trumpet takes on the function of the two trombones. The tutti violins and violas also, with the voice and the clarinets, divide these five bars into two halves. The paragraph's climax, at the middle of the three bars beginning at Fig. 129a, is one of the most memorable and finely-placed of all Strauss's innumerable $^6_4$ chords, good, bad and indifferent. Not even Stravinsky could scream at this one,[9] so asymmetrically placed in the phrase, and making D major with such sure harmonic timing the unexpected climax of a D minor paragraph. The inner-melody lines meet here and are reinforced by two trumpets, three trombones and the soft return of the drum gently rolling on the low A. For the closing four bars the descending line shadowing the voice is supported by minim chords allotted equally to mixed woodwind, brass, harps and strings, as if to tie everything up before proceeding onwards.

The last of these tutti passages comes a little later, when Elektra at last recognises the dark stranger (Figs. 144a–148a). In this vast wild upbeat to the principal lyric stretch of the work the orchestra seems to be vomiting itself up; yet the layout is rational, lucid, clean, without redundancy or sensationalism in its enforced combination of so many clashing lines. Noteworthy is the control of the overall diminution of volume after the climax at the fifth bar of Fig. 146a, by means of thinning the score as well as by individual *diminuendi*.[10] As in the three bars before Fig. 132 the Agamemnon triplets cut through from bottom to top of the heaviest brass. After the first thrust, third and fourth trombones are heard no more, after the second the bass trumpet, after the third, trumpet 1. At this point horns 6 + 8 take a short, then a long, break, to reappear only *mezzoforte* on the low E flat preparing the first, still uncertain, arrival of A flat at Fig. 148a. The first two trombones reach *piano* and cease one bar before Fig. 147a; the remaining two trumpets (2 + 3) reach *piano* and cease three bars later. The timp survives till 147a and thereafter gives only two soft isolated strokes; the tuba dies four bars later. Also at 147a the E flat clarinet is taken off, the first pair of clarinets and the two basset horns a bar later, and two bars later horns 1 + 3 and 5 + 7 stop; but the first of these pairs now doubles the first pair of clarinets (the second having been taken off meanwhile), in alternation with the basset horns and the second and third bassoons, on the rocking sixths (played in full by the strings) that wind down to Elektra's gentle re-entry on the word that, at the start of this passage, she could only cry out: her brother's name. The two lower flutes, the second oboe and the heckelphone are also severally lost during these bars; and of the other pair of horns, 2 loses his mate 4.

The mastery of such manœuvres as these is a matter at once of machine-like exactness, an experienced technique in good practice and a lively imagination for the humble human functions by which the result is actually effected. This mastery imbues everything Strauss wrote for orchestra, however perfunctory the musical substance. When, as here, the musician in him is thoroughly charged with his material, which moreover comes from the top drawer and not the bargain basement of his copious store, there is no discrepancy between technique and creation. If the whole of *Elektra* were at this level, my essay could stop here. But as I said earlier, there are places in the work where even its most masterly aspect seems to invite larger definitions of its composer's achievements and limitations.

IV

In *Elektra* a Greek drama is 'nervously' reinterpreted with all its period's mod. cons. of psychology and decadence, and clothed in music of peerless onomatopoeia that renders its every spasm and bloodfleck with naive efficiency. The work's *obvious* lapses concern Elektra's siblings: the all-too-homely effusions of Chrysothemis have already been described; the measly part for Orestes is equally contingent upon Strauss's besottedness with the soprano voice and inability to imagine fully a man's part, even when everything, from truth to Elektra's father/brother-dominated psychology to the sheer need for her to rest a bit before the final scene (and ours for relief from the work's almost-all-female tessitura), cries out for the man's music that should go with those brass chords. The two stretches when invention flags – towards the end of Elektra's long coercion of her sister, and towards the end of the duet with her brother – are pretty clear (and of course reflect the same weakness).[11]

The treatment of Aegisthus, though related, marks a different kind of lapse. It is positively surreal to hear these voluptuous Viennese waltz-strains, as if a *Sachertorte* had been delivered to the Royal Palace of Mycenae by a flunkey from M. Jourdain's entourage.[12] Though the intention is to make an obvious dramatic irony, the hand is so heavy and the incident so prolonged (Figs. 204a–212a) that the opera is all but ruined at a crucial point. The surefooted bad taste by which Strauss convinces us that his heroine *must* waltz her way to her apotheosis has here deserted him.

But these lapses are incidental. There is something subtly wrong about the work as a whole; something missing, or askew, that needs to be explored further.

It is glorious but it is not Greek! Why should we worry about this here when other instances (*Daphnis et Chloé* and *Oedipus Rex*, to take the opposite ends of the 'Greek' spectrum) raise no doubts? It is surely because, though the chastity and elevation of the original are relinquished, the work still purports to be exceedingly serious, and thus inevitably invites damaging reminders of the real thing. As always this is Hofmannsthal's fault, here in substituting neurosis and naturalistic slaughter for religiously and morally sanctified revenge.

Strauss being Strauss can only respond to this, as to everything similar, with onomatopoeia. With what remains of the original's sublimity he is ill at ease and out of his depth; whereas in the shallows that suit him he is without parallel. He can be relied upon, like a sky-ride, always to give his audience a thrill; we have to admire the generosity so eager to please, as well as the cold-blooded manipulation to which we willingly submit; together they sweep all before them. But in *Elektra* still more than in the comparable case of *Also sprach Zarathustra* we cannot miss, even while lost in admiration, the discrepancy between goal and aim that simply does not arise when his prodigious gift for music-making is attached to the completely appropriate subject. His genius for virtuosity, decoration, sumptuousness, energy and easy voluptuousness that suits *Salome* to a T can in *Elektra* seem, on a bad trip, rather appalling; and even on a good, just a shade *disappointing* – so much labour, so much skill, such resources ('the largest forces required by any opera in the repertory'), all signally failing to touch the core or sound the depth of the emotions portrayed. The cheap thrills of *Salome*[13] are certainly more successful, perhaps more elevated, because everything about the work is wired for cheap thrills. *Elektra* is wired for sublimity, and has a long way to fall.

But if not Greek, it *is* glorious! If we can once forget the subject, it is possible to enjoy Strauss at the height of his powers, using the medium he supremely understands – the orchestra (with soprano voice) – with a mastery and fullness of expression that can stand by itself as its own subject. It is disinterested, detached from causes; it is the story and character and subject-matter that are beside the point. *Elektra* is an '*orchestral* masterpiece' only, as Stravinsky said of *Jeux* (for '*trop* Lalique' we might say 'ein bisschen zu Klimt').[14] I think that for its full appreciation the heavy subject-matter and bloodiness should be made to become as diaphanous as the silly scenario of Debussy's ballet.

We could go further, and listen to *Elektra* as if it lay in the aesthetic of *L'Heure espagnole* or *Petrushka*. These works do not *pretend*; unlike *Jeux* they present no ambiguity, and can be apprehended with Latin directness. But with Strauss such detachment has to be fought for (though we see that he possesses it already), battling through the impediment of psychological profundity and other traditional pieties whose true place is elsewhere, to reach his essential content, which is authentic indeed if much simpler than appears at first sight.

He is a wizard, a conjuror, a puppet-master, a charlatan even, in the special sense whereby the charlatan in *Petrushka* brings his creatures to life for astonishment and delight, if not for pity and terror; he is the greatest master there has ever been of the *means* of music; and his vehicle is the most highly-developed machine yet produced by musical culture – the turn-of-the-century orchestra at its highest pitch of efficiency and pride.

Notes

Introduction

1 William Mann, *Richard Strauss: A Critical Study of the Operas* (London: Cassell, 1964); Norman Del Mar, *Richard Strauss: A Critical Commentary on His Life and Works*, 3 vols. (London: Barrie and Jenkins, 1978). See also Richard Specht, *Richard Strauss und sein Werk*, 2 vols. (Leipzig, Vienna and Zurich: E. P. Tal & Co., 1921), Vol. 2; Roland Tenschert, *Dreimal sieben Variationen über das Thema Richard Strauss* (Vienna: Frick, 1944); Anna Amalie Abert, *Richard Strauss: Die Opern* (Hanover: Friedrich, 1972). Michael Kennedy's *Richard Strauss* (London: Dent, 1976) is a useful introduction to the composer.

2 On *Elektra* see, for example, Ernest Newman, '*Elektra*', in *Opera Nights* (London: Putnam, 1943); Robert Craft, '*Elektra* and Richard Strauss', in *Current Convictions: Views and Reviews* (London: Secker and Warburg, 1978); Günter Schnitzler, 'Kongenialität und Divergenz: Zum Eingang der Oper *Elektra* von Hugo von Hofmannsthal und Richard Strauss', in *Dichtung und Musik*, ed. Günter Schnitzler (Stuttgart: Klett-Cotta, 1979); Peter Conrad, *Romantic Opera and Literary Form* (Berkeley: University of California Press, 1977), pp. 123–7.

3 Quoted in Craft, *Current Convictions*, p. 91. See also *Stravinsky: Selected Correspondence*, ed. Robert Craft (London: Faber. 1982), Vol. 1, p. 44n.

4 Quoted in Hans Moldenhauer, *Anton von Webern: A Chronicle of His Life and Work* (London: Gollancz, 1978), p. 148.

5 See Kim H. Kowalke, *Kurt Weill in Europe* (Ann Arbor: UMI Research Press), p. 155.

6 'Richard Strauss', *Perspectives of New Music*, Vol. 4, No. 2 (Spring–Summer 1966), pp. 118–19; see also below, p. 161, n. 4. Part of *Elektra*'s appeal for Adorno was clearly that it had influenced Berg.

7 See Bayan Northcott, 'Nicholas Maw: The Second Phase', *Musical Times*, Vol. 128, No. 1734 (August 1987), p. 433. I am grateful to Nicholas Maw, who attended these classes, for providing more information about them (private communication).

8 *Die Musik des 19. Jahrhunderts* (Wiesbaden: Akademische Verlagsgesellschaft Athenaion, 1980), pp. 291–3. See also *Realism in Nineteenth-Century Music*, trans. Mary Whittall (Cambridge: CUP, 1985), pp. 118–19.

9 'This appalling story . . . Elektra actually performs her awful dance [!] . . . a horrible waltz . . . the concentration of women's voices shrieking in

148

almost unrelieved hysteria', and so on. *Richard Strauss*, Vol. 1, pp. 294, 302, 314, 317.

10 *Die Elektra-Partitur von Richard Strauss: Ein Lehrbuch für die Technik der dramatischen Komposition* (Salzburg: Pustet, 1978). In addition there are at least four American dissertations devoted wholly or partly to the work: Norman M. Dinerstein, 'Polychordality in *Salome* and *Elektra*: A Study of the Application of Re-Interpretation Technique' (Princeton University, 1974); Lawrence F. McDonald, 'Compositional Procedures in Richard Strauss' *Elektra*' (University of Michigan, 1976); Margery A. Enix, 'The Dissolution of the Functional Harmonic Tonal System: 1850– 1910' (University of Indiana, 1977); Richard A. Kaplan, 'The Musical Language of *Elektra*: A Study in Chromatic Harmony' (University of Michigan, 1985).

11 See *Richard Strauss: 'Salome'*, ed. Derrick Puffett (Cambridge: CUP, 1989), especially the Introduction and Chapter 8 ('Critical Reception').

12 See Walter Panofsky, *Richard Strauss: Partitur eines Lebens* (Darmstadt: Deutsche Buch-Gemeinschaft, 1965), p. 143 (my translations).

13 See Max Steinitzer, *Richard Strauss* (Berlin: Schuster and Loeffler, 1911), p. 263. Steinitzer presents a fascinating selection of reviews, pp. 264–6.

14 Some of these (including the notorious 'Elektric Chair') are reproduced in Kurt Wilhelm, *Richard Strauss persönlich: Eine Bildbiographie* (Munich: Kindler, 1984), pp. 152–4.

15 See Ernst Krause, *Richard Strauss: The Man and His Work* (London: Collet, 1964), p. 310 (English titles in the original).

16 Panofsky, *Richard Strauss*, p. 144 (my translation).

17 *Ibid.*, pp. 143–4 (my translation). See also the reviews by Max Kowalski and Max Steinitzer quoted in Steinitzer, *Richard Strauss*, pp. 265–6. It seems that Strauss himself was a little frightened by the Klytämnestra scene in later life: see Panofsky, *Richard Strauss*, p. 145. On this scene see also below, pp. 82ff.

18 See Alan Jefferson, *The Operas of Richard Strauss in Britain 1910–1963* (London: Putnam, 1963), pp. 20ff. The only dissenter was Ernest Newman. His unfavourable review sparked off the famous controversy with George Bernard Shaw, reprinted in Ernest Newman, *Testament of Music* (London: Putnam, 1963), pp. 115–62. Some of the early American notices (as hostile as the early German ones) are reprinted in Nicolas Slonimsky, *Lexicon of Musical Invective: Critical Assaults on Composers since Beethoven's Time*, 2nd edn (Seattle: University of Washington Press, 1969), pp. 193–5.

19 Krause, *Richard Strauss*, pp. 304–5.

20 Donald G. Daviau and George J. Buelow, *The 'Ariadne auf Naxos' of Hugo von Hofmannsthal and Richard Strauss* (Chapel Hill: University of North Carolina Press, 1975), p. 8. The circumstances in which Strauss approached Hofmannsthal are not absolutely clear, since the relevant letter (if indeed the approach was made by letter) has not survived.

21 Wilhelm, *Richard Strauss persönlich*, p. 151.

22 See below, p. 17.

23 See *The Correspondence between Richard Strauss and Hugo von Hof-*

mannsthal, trans. Hanns Hammelmann and Ewald Osers (Cambridge: CUP, 1980), p. 2. *Der Triumph der Zeit* was later set by Alexander Zemlinsky.

24 See below, p. 28. Strauss's reminiscences (see n. 25 below) are no help: he was hopelessly vague about dates.

25 *Recollections and Reflections*, ed. Willi Schuh, trans. L. J. Lawrence (London: Boosey and Hawkes, 1953), p. 154.

26 See above, n. 20, and below, p. 28.

27 See *The Correspondence between Richard Strauss and Hugo von Hofmannsthal*, pp. 2–3.

28 Letter of 27 April 1906, in *ibid.*, p. 4.

29 There was more than flattery involved here, however. This was a classic aesthetic position derived from Schopenhauer, one which Hofmannsthal might have known would appeal to Strauss. See below, pp. 41–3.

30 See *The Correspondence between Richard Strauss and Hugo von Hofmannsthal*, p. 7.

31 See pp. 28–31.

32 Steinitzer (*Richard Strauss*, p. 89) and Wilhelm (*Richard Strauss persönlich*, p. 152) opt for the monologue; Mann (*Richard Strauss*, p. 71), Panofsky (*Richard Strauss*, p. 145) and Kennedy ('Richard Strauss', in *The New Grove Dictionary of Music and Musicians*, ed. Stanley Sadie, 20 vols. (London: Macmillan, 1980), Vol. 18, p. 229) for the Klytämnestra scene. Steinitzer is perhaps the most likely to be right, as he was writing so close to the time of composition.

33 Strauss said it was the last thing he played to him. See *Gustav Mahler–Richard Strauss: Correspondence 1888–1911*, ed. with notes and an essay by Herta Blaukopf, trans. Edmund Jephcott (London: Faber, 1984), p. 151.

34 Letter to Alma Mahler, quoted in *ibid.*, p. 146.

35 Many years later Strauss wrote in his diary: 'My boldest passage harmonically is perhaps Clytemnestra's day-dream [*sic*] narrative where the pedal-note has the function of nightmare. A piece which even Mahler . . . could not accept.' Quoted in *ibid.*, p. 151.

36 See below, pp. 31–2.

37 See Steinitzer, *Richard Strauss*, pp. 91–2.

38 See his letter to Strauss of 7 October 1908, in *The Correspondence between Richard Strauss and Hugo von Hofmannsthal*, pp. 24–5.

39 Letters reproduced in Friedrich von Schuch, *Richard Strauss, Ernst von Schuch und Dresdens Oper*, 2nd edn (Leipzig: Verlag der Kunst, 1953), pp. 82–4. Translations from Krause, *Richard Strauss*, p. 311.

40 See Strauss's 'Reminiscences of the First Performance of My Operas', p. 156; also the reminiscences of Schumann-Heinck reproduced in Panofsky, *Richard Strauss*, pp. 145–6.

41 'Reminiscences of the First Performance of My Operas', p. 156.

42 *The Correspondence between Richard Strauss and Hugo von Hofmannsthal*, p. 29.

43 See *Richard Strauss: 'Salome'*, ed. Derrick Puffett, especially the chapters by Tethys Carpenter and Craig Ayrey.

44 'Reminiscences of the First Performance of My Operas', p. 155.

45 Some of these problems are addressed below.
46 *Richard Strauss*, p. 94.
47 See the photographs reproduced in Rudolf Hartmann, *Richard Strauss: The Staging of His Operas and Ballets*, trans. Graham Davies (Oxford: Phaidon Press, 1982), and Roland Tenschert, *Dreimal sieben Variationen über das Thema Richard Strauss*.

1 Electra's story

1 See John Herington, *Poetry into Drama* (Berkeley: University of California Press, 1985); Karl Schefold, *Myth and Legend in Early Greek Art*, trans. Audrey Hicks (London: West Germany Press, 1966). For a brief account of the epic tradition after Homer and Hesiod, see *The Cambridge History of Classical Literature*, ed. P. E. Easterling and B. M. W. Knox, Vol. 1 (Cambridge: CUP, 1985), Chapter 4.
2 *Odyssey*, Book 3, ll. 255–75, 303–5; Book 4, ll. 512–36; Book 11, ll. 385–453; Book 24, ll. 192–202.
3 *Odyssey*, Book 1, ll. 29–43, 298–302; Book 3, ll. 193–8, 306–16.
4 Most scholars would place both the Sophoclean and the Euripidean *Electra* within the period 422–410 B.C.; Euripides' *Orestes* was performed in 408. On dating, see for example Albin Lesky, *Greek Tragic Poetry*, trans. Matthew Dillon (New Haven: Yale University Press, 1983), pp. 160, 291–2, 299–300.
5 See further Sophocles, *Electra*, ed. J. C. Kamerbeek (Leiden: E. J. Brill, 1974), pp. 1–5; A. J. N. W. Prag, *The Oresteia: Iconographic and Narrative Tradition* (Warminster: Aris and Phillips, 1985), Chapter 8; Aeschylus, *Choephoroi*, ed. A. F. Garvie (Oxford: Clarendon, 1986), pp. ix–xxvi. The earliest extant mention of Electra seems to be the pseudo-Hesiodic *Catalogue of Women*, fr. 23a.16 M-W, but nothing is said of her except that she was beautiful.
6 *Orestes*, l. 72; cf. the scholion on *Orestes*, l. 22. The true meaning of the name is 'the brilliant one'; there were several other Electras in Greek myth, most notably a daughter of Ocean who became the mother of Iris; one of the seven Pleiades, the mother, by Zeus, of the Trojan Dardanus; a sister of Cadmus, King of Thebes.
7 Aelian, *Varia historia*, Book 4, l. 26 (=*Poetae Melici Graeci*, ed. D. L. Page (London: OUP, 1962), No. 700).
8 See Garvie (n. 5 above), pp. xvii–xxiv.
9 Sophocles, *Electra*, ll. 871–937.
10 Euripides, *Electra*, ll. 487–546.
11 Sophocles, *Electra*, ll. 1376–1490.
12 Euripides, *Electra*, ll. 646–98; 1165–1232, especially 1224–5. Cf. ll. 959–87 (Electra urges on the reluctant Orestes) and 998–1146 (Electra lures Clytemnestra into her home). Electra does not use an axe, whatever the weapon associated with Clytemnestra (on which see Malcolm Davies, 'Aeschylus' Clytemnestra: Sword or Axe?', *Classical Quarterly*, Vol. 37 (1987), pp. 65–71).
13 *Electra*, ll. 1249, 1340–1; *Orestes*, ll. 1092–3, 1207–8, 1658–9; cf. *Iphigenia in Tauris*, ll. 695–6, 716, 915. This was evidently important in some ver-

sions of the story; cf. Pausanias, *Description of Greece*, Book 2, 16.7 (quoting Hellanicus) and Book 3, 1.6, which mention the children of Electra and Pylades. The role of Pylades as Orestes' helper seems to have had a long history: cf. Proclus' summary of the epic *Nostoi* attributed to Agias of Trozen (Oxford Classical Text of Homer, Vol. 5, p. 109).

14 See *Lexicon Iconographicum Mythologiae Classicae*, Vol. 3 (Zurich and Munich, 1986), fasc. 2, *s.v.* Elektra, with Ian McPhee's commentary (Vol. 3, fasc. 1, pp. 709–19). Sometimes the god Hermes is shown with Orestes.

15 Sophocles, *Electra*, ll. 1126–70. Cf. Charles Segal, *Interpreting Greek Tragedy* (Ithaca: Cornell University Press, 1986), pp. 125–9.

16 Euripides, *Electra*, ll. 54–81; 107–49.

2 Hofmannsthal's *Elektra*: from Sophocles to Strauss

1 Hugo von Hofmannsthal, *Briefe 1900–1909* (Vienna: Bermann-Fischer Verlag, 1937), p. 52. Translations from the German are mine unless otherwise indicated. In the preceding letter, to Richard Beer-Hofmann, Hofmannsthal wrote: 'For a week now I have been working on the play based on material from Browning. In contrast to my earlier lyrical dramatic works, this time I am trying to be very restrained and to establish a very exact scenario; also an outline of ideas, an outline for each figure.' *Ibid.*, p. 52.

2 Gertrud Schlesinger was the daughter of the President of the Anglo-Austrian Bank. On 1 July 1901 they moved into the house in Rodaun, on the outskirts of Vienna, where they lived until Hofmannsthal's death in 1929.

3 'Such things as the ballet and the pantomime are actually nothing. Certain material hopes were attached to the ballet, which have however been completely dashed.' *Briefe 1900–1909*, p. 62.

4 *Ibid.*, pp. 56–7 (letter of 4 September or 4 October 1901: not all the letters are fully dated).

5 To Ria Schmujlow-Claasen he wrote on 22 December 1901: 'Since I have been married I have worked without interruption, mostly 8 to 10 hours a day. In the summer mainly on a tragedy about which I can't talk. I didn't get beyond a very exact scenario.' *Ibid.*, p. 62.

6 Konrad Kenkel, 'Die Funktion der Sprache bei Hofmannsthal vor und nach der Chandos-Krise', *Texte und Kontexte*, Vol. 11 (1973), pp. 89–101; Günther Erken, 'Hofmannsthals dramatischer Stil: Untersuchungen zur Symbolik und Dramaturgie', *Hermaea*, Vol. 20 (1967), pp. 47–8; Michael Hamburger, *Hofmannsthal: Three Essays* (Princeton: Princeton University Press, 1972), pp. 65–84. 'Der Brief des Lord Chandos' ('The Lord Chandos Letter') was published in 1902 as 'Ein Brief'. It is an essay in letter form in which the fictitious writer, Philipp Lord Chandos, seeks to explain to Francis Bacon, the father of modern scientific method, why after five productive years he has for two years been unable to write creatively. He, Lord Chandos, has in these two years come to a quasi-mystical perception of reality, which he maintains cannot be adequately

expressed in language or rationally connected thought – though he does it beautifully in the letter. It has often been assumed that this essay of Hofmannsthal's was partly autobiographical. See the extract from his letter to Rudolf Schröder quoted on p. 19.

7 *Briefe 1900–1909*, p. 76.

8 *Ibid.*, p. 150.

9 In 1835 Hofmannsthal's great-grandfather Isaak Löw Hofmann was given the title 'Edler von Hofmannsthal'. His grandfather married a Catholic and gave up the Jewish faith. The family was thoroughly assimilated by the time Hofmannsthal was born.

10 *Briefe 1900–1909*, p. 67. In a letter to Richard Dehmel he wrote: 'I find it strange myself that in many months, and months of happy concentration, not a single poem has been written.' *Ibid.*, p. 61.

11 For Hofmannsthal's own analysis of the roles of duty and social responsibility in his work, see 'Ad me ipsum (1916–1929): Eine Interpretation', in Hugo von Hofmannsthal, *Gesammelte Werke: Reden und Aufsätze III*, ed. Bernd Schoeller and Ingeborg Beyer-Ahlert (Frankfurt am Main: Fischer, 1980), pp. 599–605.

12 *Briefe 1900–1909*, p. 67.

13 German translation (*Nachtasyl*) by A. Scholz (1903).

14 Hofmannsthal may also have been influenced by Eysoldt's performance in Oscar Wilde's *Salomé*, which Reinhardt gave earlier in 1903.

15 *Briefe 1900–1909*, p. 132.

16 Erwin Rohde, *Psyche* (Freiburg: Otto Kante, 1894); Jacob Bachofen, *Das Mutterrecht*, Vols. 2 and 3 (Basel: Franz Deuticke, 1861); Hermann Bahr, *Dialog vom Tragischen* (Berlin: Verlag der literarischen Anstalt Rütten und Loening, 1904), pp. 23f.; Josef Breuer and Sigmund Freud, *Studien über Hysterie* (Vienna: Albert Langen, 1895).

17 Cf. Bernd Urban, 'Hofmannsthal, Freud und die Psychoanalyse', in *Literatur und Psychologie*, ed. Bernd Urban and Wolfram Mauser (Frankfurt am Main: Fischer, 1978), p. 34; Elisabeth Steingruber, *Hugo von Hofmannsthals Sophokleische Dramen* (Winterthur, 1956), p. 78; Edgar Herderer, *Hugo von Hofmannsthal* (Frankfurt am Main: Fischer, 1960), pp. 192–218.

18 Michael Ewans's article 'Elektra: Sophokles, von Hofmannsthal, Strauss' (*Ramus*, Vol. 13, No. 2 (1984), pp. 135–54) does rightly emphasise the closeness of Hofmannsthal to Sophocles but labours unnecessarily to prove the 'modernity' of all three authors of the work. It only remains for him to show that Sophocles had also read Breuer and Freud. Furthermore, he falls into the not uncommon error of at one point talking as if Hofmannsthal had actually written *Elektra* as a libretto – and chastising his inexperience (p. 150).

19 In his study 'Hugo von Hofmannsthals Griechenstücke', *Corona*, Vols. 12–14 (Jahresbericht 1910/12), Ernst Hladny claims that in conversation Hofmannsthal told him that at the time of writing *Elektra* he had leafed through Rohde's *Psyche* and 'the remarkable book about hysteria by Doctors Breuer and Freud'. But in May 1904 Hofmannsthal wrote to Hermann Bahr: 'Could you possibly lend (send) me for a few days the

book by Freud and Breuer about curing hysteria by releasing suppressed memories? If not, please write down the exact title for me, so that I can have it sent.' *Briefe 1900–1909*, p. 142.

20 Cf. 'Aufzeichnungen aus dem Nachlass 1904', in *Reden und Aufsätze III*, p. 452.

21 'Aufzeichnungen aus dem Nachlass 1903', in *ibid.*, p. 443.

22 Hofmannsthal preserves the unities. His play takes place between dusk and evening. This is tied in with the black and red colour-scheme of the stage design.

23 Translations are from the edition cited in n. 25.

24 'Aufzeichnungen aus dem Nachlass 1903', in *ibid.*, p. 443.

25 For example:

SOPHOCLES
(*Electra and Other Plays*, trans. E. F. Watling (Harmondsworth: Penguin, 1953))

HOFMANNSTHAL
(*Dramen II*, ed. Bernd Schoeller (Frankfurt am Main: Fischer, 1979))

ELECTRA
I am beside myself. (l. 223)

CHRYSOTHEMIS (*to Electra*)
Du bist wie ausser dir. (p. 215)
[You are beside yourself.]

ELECTRA
Each night that dies with dawn
I bring my sad songs here
And tear my breast until it bleeds.
(ll. 88–90)

ZWEITE DIENERIN
. . . Ist doch ihre Stunde,
die Stunde wo sie um den Vater heult,
dass alle Wände schallen. (p. 187)

[It is her hour, / the hour when she cries for her father / so that the walls resound.]

ELECTRA
Strike her again, strike! (l. 1415)

ELEKTRA
Triff noch einmal! (p. 229)
[Strike again!]

ELECTRA
Then I must do the thing myself, alone,
For done it must be. (ll. 1012–13)

ELEKTRA
Nun denn allein! (p. 219)
[Alone then!]

ELECTRA (*to Chrysothemis*)
. . . call yourself mother's daughter
Then everyone will know you for what you are. (ll. 363–4)

ELEKTRA (*to Chrysothemis*)
Was willst du, Tochter meiner Mutter?
(p. 192)

[What do you want, daughter of my mother?]

ELECTRA
. . . a skulking villain,
A coward hiding behind a woman's skirts. (ll. 301–2)

ELEKTRA (*of Aegisth*)
. . . jenes andre Weib, die Memme, ei
Aegisth, der tapfre Meuchelmörder, er,
der Heldentaten nur im Bett vollführt.
(p. 192)

[. . . that other woman, the cissy, / Aegisthus, the bold assassin, he / who performs heroic deeds only in bed.]

26 'Aufzeichnungen aus dem Nachlass 1903', in *Reden und Aufsätze III*, p. 443.

27 Reference is to the edition cited in n. 25.

28 But Hofmannsthal was strangely reluctant to write 'Elektra stirbt'. The stage directions say only that she collapses and lies rigid (p. 234).

29 'Aufzeichnungen aus dem Nachlass 1903', in *Reden und Aufsätze III*, p. 444.

30 'Ad me ipsum', in *ibid.*, pp. 602–3. The 'Abenteurer' is a reference to Hofmannsthal's play *Der Abenteurer und die Sängerin*.

31 'Aufzeichnungen aus dem Nachlass 1905', in *ibid.*, p. 461.

32 *Briefe 1900–1909*, p. 170.

33 Aeschylus also takes up the themes of memory and forgetting, which are central to Hofmannsthal's characterisation of Elektra and Chrysothemis. Aeschylus, *Agamemnon*, trans. Robert Fagles (Harmondsworth: Penguin, 1977), ll. 177–82.

34 Aeschylus, *The Libation Bearers*, trans. Robert Fagles (Harmondsworth: Penguin, 1977), ll. 298, 75, 31, 465.

35 He certainly saw *a* performance (see Strauss's *Recollections and Reflections*, ed. Willi Schuh, trans. L. J. Lawrence (London: Boosey and Hawkes, 1953), p. 154). He also saw Gertrud Eysoldt in Wilde's *Salomé* (*ibid.*, p. 150).

36 Del Mar gives the incorrect date of 1903–4. *Richard Strauss: A Critical Commentary on His Life and Works*, 3 vols. (London: Barrie and Jenkins, 1978), Vol. 1, p. 289.

37 *Briefe 1900–1909*, p. 221. *Ödipus und die Sphinx*, a three-act verse tragedy based on J. Peladans' *Oedipe et le sphinx*, was the first part of an uncompleted trilogy.

38 *The Correspondence between Richard Strauss and Hugo von Hofmannsthal*, trans. Hanns Hammelmann and Ewald Osers (Cambridge: CUP, 1980), p. 5.

39 *Ibid.*, p. 6. Hofmannsthal added that since he was forgoing substantial immediate rights he wished to ask for an advance of two thousand marks, a fairly large sum.

40 *Briefe 1900–1909*, p. 305.

41 That is, the *Gesammelte Werke in Einzelausgaben: Dramen II*, ed. Herbert Steiner (Frankfurt am Main: Fischer, 1954), p. 531, and the more recent Bernd Schoeller edition used here.

42 ELEKTRA   Traumbild, mir geschenktes
        Traumbild, schöner als alle Träume!
        Hehres, unbegreifliches, erhabenes Gesicht,
        o bleib bei mir! Lös nicht
        in Luft dich auf, vergeh mir nicht,
        es sei denn, dass ich jetzt gleich
        sterben muss und du dich anzeigst
        und mich holen kommst: dann sterbe ich
        seliger, als ich gelebt! (pp. 237–8)

        Apparition, apparition / sent to me, more
        beautiful than all dreams! / Noble, incomprehensible, sublime face, / stay with me!
        Do not / dissolve into air, do not fade
        away from me, / unless I am soon / to die
        and you are showing yourself / and coming to fetch me: then I'll die / happier than
        I lived.

[Hofmannsthal originally wrote 'entzückendes Gesicht' rather than 'erhabenes Gesicht', but Strauss changed the word for musical reasons. See Del Mar, *Richard Strauss*, Vol. 1, p. 323. Ed.]

43 The occasional uncertainties, the slight ambivalence towards the heroine herself and the awkward thematic embellishments of Hofmannsthal's Sophocles adaptation perhaps arose because Hofmannsthal wrote in an age which on the whole tended to deny tragedy (rather than, say, to transcend it, which was Goethe's aim) and to treat the external world only as metaphor. This was possibly Hofmannsthal's own tragedy. While he could improve his grasp of dramatic construction at Sophocles' feet, no amount of sitting there would ever have brought it home to him that matricide is not only metaphor but also murder, and that when it is *justifiable* matricide this is what tragedy means.

44 *Briefe 1900–1909*, p. 241.
45 *Ibid.*, p. 313.
46 *Ibid.*, p. 336.
47 *Ibid.*, p. 357.

3 The music of *Elektra*: some preliminary thoughts

1 Hugo von Hofmannsthal, *Elektra: Tragödie in einem Aufzug frei nach Sophokles*, in *Gesammelte Werke: Dramen II*, ed. Bernd Schoeller (Frankfurt am Main: Fischer, 1979), pp. 190–1, 222.

2 See Günter Schnitzler, 'Kongenialität und Divergenz: Zum Eingang der Oper *Elektra* von Hugo von Hofmannsthal und Richard Strauss', in *Dichtung und Musik*, ed. Günter Schnitzler (Stuttgart: Klett-Cotta, 1979), p. 190, on the symbolic meaning of names for Hofmannsthal. Norman Del Mar makes the point in a different way:

It was a feature of Hofmannsthal's text that the name of Agamemnon was never spoken by anyone, as if it were taboo in the house of his slaughter. Not even in Elektra's soliloquy does she address him by name . . . It is Orestes who finally breaks the spell in the drama, and then Elektra, with a fine sense of climax, hurls the name in the face of Aegisthus as he is being murdered. Such subtlety Strauss felt to be merely abstruse in the case of a music drama, where it is above all important that the action should be crystal clear at every point. He was particularly obsessed, moreover, by the idea of the spirit of Agamemnon hanging like a cloud over the entire situation . . . Strauss accordingly reverses Hofmannsthal's intention to the very utmost, introducing the majestic name on every possible occasion and framing the score in its opening and closing pages with a motif based directly upon it.

Richard Strauss: A Critical Commentary on His Life and Works, 3 vols. (London: Barrie and Jenkins, 1978), Vol. 1, pp. 297–8. As Schnitzler observes, it is astonishing that Hofmannsthal seems not to have commented upon this change.

3 The monologue is analysed in detail in Richard A. Kaplan, 'The Musical Language of *Elektra*: A Study in Chromatic Harmony' (Unpublished Ph.D. Diss., University of Michigan, 1985), pp. 117–70, and, more briefly,

in Carl Dahlhaus, *Die Musik des 19. Jahrhunderts* (Wiesbaden: Akademische Verlagsgesellschaft Athenaion, 1980), p. 293.
4 Hofmannsthal, *Elektra*, pp. 193–4. In both play and libretto the speech is interrupted by Elektra's sarcastic 'Mit wem?' ('On whom [should I have pity]?') and 'Armes Geschöpf!' ('You poor creature!').
5 Translations are from the booklet that accompanies the Solti recording (Decca SET 354–5).
6 These changes and others are discussed in Jakob Knaus, *Hofmannsthals Weg zur Oper 'Die Frau ohne Schatten': Rücksichte und Einflüsse auf die Musik* (Berlin: de Gruyter, 1971), pp. 12–29. Knaus, however, says little about the musical consequences of the changes.
7 Given above, p. 155, n. 42.
8 In his 'Reminiscences of the First Performance of My Operas' Strauss tried to take sole credit for the change, almost as if he had written the new lines himself: 'When I first saw Hofmannsthal's inspired play . . . I immediately recognised, of course, what a magnificent operatic libretto it might be (after the alteration I made in the Orestes scene it has actually become one) . . .' *Recollections and Reflections*, ed. Willi Schuh, trans. L. J. Lawrence (London: Boosey and Hawkes, 1953), p. 154.
9 So much for the idea that the work is a *Literaturoper*. For more on this subject, see my article 'Some Reflections on *Literaturoper*', *German Life and Letters*, Vol. 35, No. 3 (April 1982).
10 It was certainly Strauss's response to the text of *Salome*: see *Richard Strauss: 'Salome'*, ed. Derrick Puffett (Cambridge: CUP, 1989), especially the chapter by Tethys Carpenter.
11 The earliest leitmotive guide to the work seems to have been Otto Röse and Julius Prüwer, *Elektra: Ein Musikführer durch das Werk* (Berlin: Fürstner, 1909). This could claim a certain authority, as it was produced by Strauss's own publishers. Other early guides were Ernst Fischer-Planer, *Einführung in die Musik von Richard Strauss und Elektra* (Leipzig: Reform, 1909) and E. Hutcheson, *Elektra by Richard Strauss: A Guide to the Opera with Musical Examples from the Score* (New York, 1910). The familiar discussions of the work by William Mann (*Richard Strauss: A Critical Study of the Operas* (London: Cassell, 1964), pp. 77–94) and Norman Del Mar (*Richard Strauss*, Vol. 1, pp. 296–331) adopt a leitmotivic approach. See also the lists of leitmotives in Kurt Overhoff, *Die Elektra-Partitur von Richard Strauss: Ein Lehrbuch für die Technik der dramatischen Komposition* (Salzburg: Pustet, 1978), pp. 195–205, and in Margery A. Enix, 'The Dissolution of the Functional Harmonic Tonal System: 1850–1910' (Unpublished Ph.D. Diss., University of Indiana, 1977), pp. 369–74. The limitations of this approach are discussed in my essay '*Salome* as Music Drama', in *Richard Strauss: 'Salome'*.
12 Reproduced in Franz Trenner, *Die Skizzenbücher von Richard Strauss aus dem Richard-Strauss-Archiv in Garmisch* (Tutzing: Schneider, 1977), p. 163, and transcribed in Bryan Gilliam, 'Strauss's Preliminary Opera Sketches: Thematic Fragments and Symphonic Continuity', *Nineteenth-Century Music*, Vol. 9, No. 3 (Spring 1986), p. 180. The sketches for *Elektra* are in Sketchbooks 17, 18 and 19, held in the Richard-Strauss-Archiv at Garmisch (see Trenner, *Skizzenbücher*, pp. 28–32, together

with the facsimiles on pp. 163–5). The particular sketch in question is folio 1 of Sketchbook 17. More *Elektra* sketches are transcribed on pp. 182–5 of Gilliam's article.

13 The fate of this particular motive, possibly the first that occurred to Strauss, is curious. Given its name (one of the composer's more 'old-fashioned' labellings), we might have expected it to appear on almost every page of the score. But this role seems to have passed to the Agamemnon motive. The motive of 'the fate of the house of Atreus' appears only twice, to my knowledge: at Figs. 122/2–3 (when Chrysothemis says that Klytämnestra has dreamt of Orestes) and 213a/4–6 (the moment of Aegisthus' death). In neither case is it particularly conspicuous. At some point in the creative process it seems to have transformed itself into the Orestes motive; but if that is the case, it is odd that Strauss saw fit to include the early version in the score at all, and then in such a desultory fashion.

14 See pp. 110–15.

15 Strauss actually talks of its 'unending climaxes'. 'Reminiscences of the First Performance of My Operas', p. 154.

16 List adapted from Del Mar, *Richard Strauss*, Vol. 1, p. 296.

17 *Die Elektra-Partitur von Richard Strauss*, p. 74. See also Mann, *Richard Strauss*, p. 89.

18 There is also a change of metre and of tempo. It is curious that the first $\frac{3}{4}$ bar is incomplete: the result is an uncomfortable crashing of gears, suggesting that Strauss was not altogether happy with a break at this point. According to Ernst Krause (who discusses the composer's fondness for the one-act form), Strauss 'often remarked in later years that the caesura at the end of an act disturbed him': *Richard Strauss: The Man and His Work* (London: Collet, 1964), p. 302.

19 See Mann, *Richard Strauss*, p. 384.

20 Though Chrysothemis' final cadence, at the very end of the opera, refers to Elektra's final cadence in the Klytämnestra scene (three bars before Fig. 259).

21 'Reminiscences of the First Performance of My Operas', p. 154.

22 'Kongenialität und Divergenz', p. 177.

23 This is the only part of the score that recalls Adorno's gibe: 'Like his predecessor, Berlioz, [Strauss] wrote display-music on a worldwide scale – World's Fair Music'. 'Richard Strauss', *Perspectives of New Music*, Vol. 4, No. 1 (Fall–Winter 1965), p. 23.

24 See Carolyn Abbate's discussion of this passage, pp. 107, 125–6 below.

25 Robert Craft observes that, in these closing pages, Chrysothemis becomes vocally indistinguishable from her sister: '*Elektra* and Richard Strauss', in *Current Convictions: Views and Reviews* (London: Secker and Warburg, 1978), p. 149.

26 Strauss wrote of the first performance:

I was beginning to realise at that time how fundamentally my vocal style differs even from that of Wagner. My vocal style has the pace of a stage play and frequently comes into conflict with the figuring and polyphony of the orchestra, so that none but the best conductors, who themselves know something of singing, can establish the balance of volume and speed between singer and baton. The struggle between word and music has been the problem of my life right from the beginning, which *Capriccio* solves with a question mark.

'Reminiscences of the First Performance of My Operas', p. 156.
27 Egon Wellesz argues that it is in fact vitiated by the power of Elektra's monologue, which makes the finale seem an anticlimax. *Essays on Opera*, trans. Patricia Kean (London: Dennis Dobson, 1950), pp. 113–14.
28 Hans Keller's phrase. An example of 'overlapping' structures in *Elektra* might be the way Klytämnestra's description of her dream (Fig. 177ff.) merges into the later part of the scene. Despite the assertion of B minor, the predominant tonality of the dream description, at Fig. 193, there is no V–I cadence, as if the passage were deliberately left incomplete. The first such cadence after this point is in fact in C minor (Fig. 200). Thereafter, though B minor continues to exert an influence – cf. Figs. 194/4, 203, 218/5, 224, 228 – it is gradually displaced by C (the all-important change of key signature comes at 229/10). C minor dominates the last part of the scene but is in turn displaced by B flat at Fig. 259 (see Chapter 5, Ex. 5). It is only in the subsequent interlude that B (now major) is restored.
29 Klytämnestra's dream description could be said to be 'in' B minor, since it prolongs the triad over an extended passage; but it does not actually have a V–I cadence. (See the previous note.)
30 'A "Beautiful Coloured, Musical Thing"' (*Salome*), in *Current Convictions*, p. 129.
31 '*Elektra* and Richard Strauss', p. 151.
32 See Robert Bailey, 'The Structure of the *Ring* and Its Evolution', *Nineteenth-Century Music*, Vol. 1 (1977), pp. 51–3. On associative tonality in *Salome*, see my postscript to Roland Tenschert's essay 'Strauss as Librettist', in *Richard Strauss: 'Salome'*. Associative tonality (or 'motivic tonality', as he prefers to call it) in *Elektra* is discussed in Kaplan, 'The Musical Language of *Elektra*: A Study in Chromatic Harmony', p. 123.
33 Gilliam, 'Strauss's Preliminary Opera Sketches', p. 178.
34 *Die Elektra-Partitur von Richard Strauss*, p. 7.
35 'Wagner's Later Stage Works', in *The New Oxford History of Music, Vol. 9: Romanticism*, ed. Gerald Abraham (London: OUP, 1989). I am grateful to Arnold Whittall for letting me see his article in typescript.
36 His conception of tonality – again, as opposed to his actual practice – was simplistic too, but this is a subject for a separate essay. It seems appropriate to mention, however, that a note in Sketchbook 17, probably referring to *Elektra*, says: 'Purity C major . . . heroic theme E flat major . . .' (Trenner, *Skizzenbücher*, p. 29). These are entirely traditional associations, which have a historical interest as well as an analytical one.
37 Enix observes that Strauss also avoids key signatures using more than three accidentals: 'The Dissolution of the Functional Harmonic Tonal System: 1850–1910', p. 375.

38 See n. 36 above!
39 One of the oddest attempts to prove that Strauss was a conservative is that of Edward Wright Murphy, who presents a mass of statistical evidence (mostly simple chord descriptions) to support his case: 'Harmony and Tonality in the Large Orchestral Works of Richard Strauss' (Unpublished Ph.D. Diss., University of Indiana, 1963), quoted in Sherrill Hahn Pantle, *'Die Frau ohne Schatten' by Hugo von Hofmannsthal and Richard Strauss: An Analysis of Text, Music and Their Relationship* (Berne: Lang, 1978), p. 224.
40 See Del Mar, *Richard Strauss*, Vol. 1, p. 311, n. 14.
41 Carolyn Abbate's apt word. See below, p. 107.
42 '*Elektra* and Richard Strauss', p. 149.
43 See 'Reminiscences of the First Performance of My Operas', p. 154; also the anonymous 'Richard Strauss' *Elektra*', *Allgemeine Musikzeitung* [Berlin], 25 September 1908, p. 669.
44 All the same, it is odd to find Strauss writing: 'I am almost tempted to say that [*Elektra*] is to *Salome* what the more flawless, and stylistically more uniform *Lohengrin* is to the inspired first venture of *Tannhäuser*'. 'Reminiscences of the First Performance of My Operas', p. 155.
45 *The Correspondence between Richard Strauss and Hugo von Hofmannsthal*, trans. Hanns Hammelmann and Ewald Osers (Cambridge: CUP, 1980), p. 16.
46 Arthur Schopenhauer, *The World as Will and Representation*, trans. E. F. J. Payne (New York: Dover, 1958), Vol. 2, pp. 448–9 (my emphasis).
47 See Willi Schuh, *Richard Strauss: A Chronicle of the Early Years (1864–1898)*, trans. Mary Whittall (Cambridge: CUP, 1982), pp. 118, 285, 308–13.
48 Curiously, Ernest Newman wrote after a performance of *Der Rosenkavalier* in 1913:

> One came away wishing that Strauss would now separate himself from the theatre, that has done him so much harm as well as good during his ten years' association with it, and concentrate upon some purely orchestral work that would call out all the best that is in him, and the form of which would force him to think concentratedly, because there would be no stage action to keep us uncritically occupied while he was merely cleverly marking time in the orchestra.

Article in the *Birmingham Post*, reprinted in *Testament of Music* (London: Putnam, 1963), p. 110.
49 'Hofmannsthal's *Elektra*: From Drama to Libretto', in *Elektra*, ed. Nicholas John (London: John Calder, 1988). I am grateful to Kenneth Segar for letting me see his article in typescript. On Hofmannsthal's 'scepticism about the efficacy of language' see also above, p. 152, n. 6.
50 'Hugo von Hofmannsthals "Elektra": Geburt der Tragödie aus dem Geiste der Psychopathologie', *Deutsche Vierteljahresschrift für Literaturwissenschaft und Geistesgeschichte*, Vol. 47 (1973), quoted in Segar, 'Hofmannsthal's *Elektra*'.
51 See the quotation in n. 26 above.

4 Synopsis

1 The sections of this chapter correspond to the 'scenes' of the opera (see above, p. 36: there is of course no formal division into scenes). Quotations from the libretto are given in English only; unless otherwise stated, the translation is that which accompanies the Solti recording (Decca SET 354–5). Other synopses can be found in Ernest Newman, *Opera Nights* (London: Putnam, 1943), pp. 148–61; William Mann, *Richard Strauss: A Critical Study of the Operas* (London: Cassell, 1964), pp. 77–94; Norman Del Mar, *Richard Strauss: A Critical Commentary on His Life and Works*, 3 vols. (London: Barrie and Jenkins, 1978), Vol. 1, pp. 296–331.

2 See the ground-plan that Hofmannsthal drew for Strauss, reproduced in *The Correspondence between Richard Strauss and Hugo von Hofmannsthal*, trans. Hanns Hammelmann and Ewald Osers (Cambridge: CUP, 1980), p. 17, and, in clearer form, in Mann, *Richard Strauss*, p. 71.

3 See above, pp. 20, 24; 156, n. 2.

4 'Richard Strauss', *Perspectives of New Music*, Vol. 4, No. 2 (Spring–Summer 1966), pp. 115, 114. Adorno's corollary, that 'in return, the endings slip away from him', is more debatable. In the same article he called the Klytämnestra scene the 'climax of Strauss's work' (*ibid.*, pp. 115, 119).

5 On the 'conversational style' (not a term used by Strauss) see Wolfgang Winterhager, *Zur Struktur des Operndialogs: Komparative Analysen des musikdramatischen Werks von Richard Strauss* (Frankfurt: Lang, 1984), pp. 19–27.

6 In Hofmannsthal's play Elektra is described (in a stage direction) as being 'alone with the spots of red light that fall diagonally out of the branches of the fig-tree onto the ground and onto the walls like blood-stains'. *Elektra: Tragödie in einem Aufzug frei nach Sophokles*, in *Gesammelte Werke: Dramen II*, ed. Bernd Schoeller (Frankfurt am Main: Fischer, 1979), p. 190 (my translation).

7 *Pace* Wellesz: see *Essays on Opera*, trans. Patricia Kean (London: Dennis Dobson, 1950), p. 114.

8 See the more detailed description of this passage above, p. 34.

9 Translation adapted from the vocal score.

10 Translation adapted from the vocal score.

11 It is less sudden in Hofmannsthal's play. In a passage that Strauss omitted, Klytämnestra reminisces sentimentally about Agamemnon, so that the transition to Orestes seems more natural. *Elektra*, pp. 205–7.

12 See above, p. 29.

13 Cf. Adorno:

Strauss's productive power realizes itself in pictures, tightly packed moments. His ability to compress the plenitude of emotions, including those which are incompatible, into isolated complexes, to fit the up and down oscillation of feeling into a single instant, has no prototype, with the possible exception of the paradoxical equilibrium between delight and horror at the end of the first act of *Tristan*. In the dissonant chord of recognition from *Elektra*, there is concentrated a wealth of musical antagonisms truly beyond the reach of words. The stylistic near-impossibility of leaving just this complex chord trembling on the sweet A flat-major field seems to succeed, as though the energy which the chord stores up in itself then streams out into the resolution. 'Richard Strauss', pp. 117–18.

The chord is analysed below, p. 105. See also Richard A. Kaplan, 'The Musical Language of *Elektra*: A Study in Chromatic Harmony' (Unpublished Ph.D. Diss., University of Michigan, 1985), pp. 108–16.

14 See above, p. 42.
15 See *The Correspondence between Richard Strauss and Hugo von Hofmannsthal*, p. 18.

5 Dramatic structure and tonal organisation

1 *The Correspondence between Richard Strauss and Hugo von Hofmannsthal*, trans. Hanns Hammelmann and Ewald Osers (Cambridge: CUP, 1980), p. 3; see also above, p. 4.
2 *Ibid.*, p. 4.
3 See Bryan Gilliam, 'Strauss's Preliminary Opera Sketches: Thematic Fragments and Symphonic Continuity', *Nineteenth-Century Music*, Vol. 9, No. 3 (Spring 1986), p. 184.
4 Norman Del Mar, *Richard Strauss: A Critical Commentary on His Life and Works*, 3 vols. (London: Barrie and Jenkins, 1978), Vol. 1, p. 242.
5 *Ibid.*, pp. 301–2.
6 *Ibid.*, p. 306.
7 'Strauss's Preliminary Opera Sketches', p. 177.
8 *Ibid.*, p. 184.
9 Translations of the libretto are my own.
10 See below, pp. 82ff.
11 For a different interpretation of this passage, see below, pp. 121–4. [Ed.]
12 And see below, p. 99. [Ed.]

6 The musical language of *Elektra*

1 *Arnold Schoenberg: Letters*, ed. Erwin Stein, trans. Eithne Wilkins and Ernst Kaiser (London: Faber, 1964), p. 51.
2 Donald Mitchell, *The Language of Modern Music* (London: Faber, 1963), p. 31.
3 Strauss, 'Reminiscences of the First Performance of My Operas', in *Recollections and Reflections*, ed. Willi Schuh, trans. L. J. Lawrence (London: Boosey and Hawkes, 1953), p. 155.
4 See above, pp. 36, 57–8.
5 Ernst Krause, *Richard Strauss: The Man and his Work* (London: Collet, 1984), p. 309.
6 See above, pp. 39–40. It is well known from the sketchbooks that Strauss thought in terms of referential keys from the outset; Krause also quotes a note from the back of a sketchbook to *Elektra* which specifies:

'Elektra alone B flat minor, against the world heightened B minor. Agamemnon B flat minor, Triumph Dance C major.' *Richard Strauss*, pp. 163–4.

7 These numbers refer to pitch-class sets in the nomenclature found in
Allen Forte, *The Structure of Atonal Music* (New Haven: Yale University
Press, 1973), Appendix 1. For readers who are unfamiliar with this
system of identification, it will help to know that pitch-class sets are col-
lections of pitches from which order and register have been abstracted.
Sets of the same class (identified by the same label) share certain inter-
vallic properties and can be related under the operations of transposition
or transposition coupled with inversion. Set classes are identified by two
numbers separated by a hyphen: the first indicates the number of pitch
classes in the collection, the second the position of the set class on Forte's
list. The precise pitch-class content of each set is denoted by a number in
square brackets ([0,1,4,6,9], etc.). Such numbers are derived by collapsing
the relevant sonority into the smallest possible space (which will always
be less than an octave) and counting the lowest pitch as 0, the pitch a
semitone higher as 1, and so on up to 11. If inversion is involved, then 0
will naturally refer to the highest pitch, 1 the semitone below, and so on.

8 First reported in Max Steinitzer, *Richard Strauss* (Berlin: Schuster and
Loeffler, 1911), p. 143.

9 On the 'Elektra chord' see also Kurt Overhoff, *Die Elektra-Partitur
von Richard Strauss: Ein Lehrbuch für die Technik der dramatischen
Komposition* (Salzburg: Pustet, 1978), pp. 32–45; Richard A. Kaplan,
'The Musical Language of *Elektra*: A Study in Chromatic Harmony'
(Unpublished Ph.D. Diss., University of Michigan, 1985), pp. 96–103,
155–69.

10 There are other versions of Elektra's chord: at Fig. 232, for instance, the
bass is a major third out, giving the non-bitonal set [0,1,2,5,8], 5-Z38,
instead of 5-32, which is used at three different pitch levels (see Ex. 16).

Example 16

232

Ich hör ihn durch die   Zim-mer gehn,

[1,0,11,8,5]
[0,1,2,5,8]
1₁ 5-Z38

This would suggest that the chord was not as immutable an object as
Kaplan would have it.

11 Kaplan examines this and similar passages at some length (*ibid.*, pp. 99–
103) and comes to the curious conclusion that because it has been split
up in a random fashion (at Fig. 114/8 as [0,1,4] in parallel), [0,1,4,6,9]
is not bitonal. Surely the point here is that despite the interim segmentations the chord itself returns – on the strong beat – transposed but in just
as blatant a form as before.

12 This is what Dinerstein ('Polychordality in *Salome* and *Elektra*: A Study
of the Application of Re-Interpretation Technique' (Unpublished Ph.D.
Diss., Princeton University, 1974), pp. 29–31) calls *Umdeutungstechnik*

or reinterpretation technique, a method Strauss apparently admitted was exceptionally helpful.

13 Nor are [0,1,4,6,9] or [0,1,3,6,7,9]: both Elektra and Klytämnestra have thematic leitmotives whose appearances may or may not coincide with those of their chords. The only exception here is Orestes' Ex. 9d, which functions both as harmonic progression and as symbol. It might be noted here that there are few thematic leitmotives of any importance in *Elektra*; the significant material is always harmonic/chordal.

14 Translations are from the booklet that accompanies the Solti recording (Decca SET 354–5).

15 *Richard Strauss: A Critical Commentary on His Life and Works*, 3 vols. (London: Barrie and Jenkins, 1978), Vol. 1, p. 309.

16 From a letter by Strauss to Hofmannsthal dated 3 May 1928: 'After all, what is the so-called external framework of *Tristan*? Meaningful is only what Wagner put into it.' *The Correspondence between Richard Strauss and Hugo von Hofmannsthal*, trans. Hanns Hammelmann and Ewald Osers (Cambridge: CUP, 1980), p. 474.

17 Cf. the discussion of this passage above, p. 40. [Ed.]

18 Its prevalence is perhaps one explanation for the almost complete avoidance of the hitherto ubiquitous $^6_4$ chord, Strauss's habitual stand-by in *Salome*; here there is no room for undirected dominants.

19 Cf. Arnold Whittall above, p. 68. [Ed.]

20 It is agonising at this point because of the alternation of the cadential motive (Ex. 9g(i)), whose bass has previously descended. In fact the juxtaposition of C minor and C major has been well prepared, both by the ambivalent modality of the dance music (introduced at Fig. 53) and by Elektra's own uncertainty at cadences (for example, Fig. 61/5).

21 It is notable that all Elektra's pronouncements either to or concerning Orestes come to rest on either D or A, often spanning the fifth, and whatever the harmonisation. [Cf. Carolyn Abbate above, pp. 117ff. Ed.]

22 Cf. Adorno's remarks quoted above, pp. 161–2, n. 13.

7 Elektra's voice: music and language in Strauss's opera

1 Translations of the libretto are my own.

2 Roland Barthes, 'Listening', in *The Responsibility of Forms*, trans. Richard Howard (Oxford: Basil Blackwell, 1986), p. 249.

3 Ernst Krause, *Richard Strauss: The Man and His Work* (London, 1969), p. 305. According to Krause, Hofmannsthal admitted – sincerely or tactfully – that the music 'added to' the play and was not, therefore, merely a neutral setting of text: *ibid.*, p. 307.

4 For a proposal of methodology for interpreting *Literaturoper* see Ulrich Weisstein, 'Librettology: The Fine Art of Coping with a Chinese Twin', *Komparatistische Hefte*, Vol. 5, No. 6 (Bayreuth, 1982), pp. 36–42.

5 I have here translated Bakhtin's notion of polyglossia in the novel – artistic discourse speaking in many voices or styles of language – into musical terms (though not those implied by Bakhtin's own use of musical imagery); see, for example, M. M. Bakhtin, 'The Prehistory of Novelistic Discourse', in *The Dialogic Imagination: Four Essays*, trans. Caryl Emer-

son and Michael Holquist (Austin: University of Texas Press, 1981), pp. 41–51, 82–3.

6 The word 'heraus' was omitted in Strauss's setting.

7 Edward T. Cone, *The Composer's Voice* (Berkeley: University of California Press, 1974), pp. 57–8.

8 Richard Specht, *Richard Strauss und sein Werk*, Vol. 2 (Leipzig: E. P. Tal, 1921), p. 179 (my translation).

9 Kurt Overhoff, *Die Elektra-Partitur von Richard Strauss: Ein Lehrbuch für die Technik der dramatischen Komposition* (Salzburg: Pustet, 1978), p. 32 (my translation).

10 *Ibid.*

11 Elaine Showalter, 'The Unmanning of the Mayor of Casterbridge', in *Critical Approaches to the Fiction of Thomas Hardy*, ed. Dale Kramer (London: Macmillan, 1979), p. 102.

12 Hofmannsthal seemed to have promulgated, in some senses, this reading of the character in his later comments on the play; he wrote, for example, both of her encompassing the entire house of Atreus and of her being unable to act or bring forth life and continuation. *Gesammelte Werke: Prosa III* (Frankfurt am Main: Fischer, 1964), p. 354.

13 Arnold Whittall, 'The Music', in Lucy Beckett, *Parsifal* (Cambridge: CUP, 1981), p. 63; happily, Whittall notes that 'if human, the analyst can rarely exclude all discussion of meaning from his technical commentary'.

14 Specht, *Richard Strauss*, Vol. 2, p. 179.

15 See the definition in Umberto Eco, 'Producing Signs', in *On Signs*, ed. Marshall Blonsky (Baltimore: John Hopkins University Press, 1985), p. 176; in Eco's terms the orchestral representation of Elektra's mourning voice is a 'stylisation' produced by ostension (in the sense of quotation).

16 See, for example, Specht, *Richard Strauss*, Vol. 2, pp. 202–3.

17 A notable exception is Carl Dahlhaus, 'Wagners "Kunst des Übergangs": der Zweigesang in "Tristan und Isolde"', in *Zur musikalischen Analyse*, ed. G. Schuhmacher (Darmstadt: Wissenschaftliche Buchgesellschaft, 1963), pp. 475–86.

18 The *locus classicus* among Dahlhaus's writings on the subject is 'Formprinzipien in Wagners "Ring des Nibelungen"', in *Beiträge zur Geschichte der Oper*, ed. Heinz Becker (Regensburg: Bosse, 1969), pp. 95–129.

19 That this rather flat view of operatic music – attractive as it may be to tidy critical imaginations – is erroneously attributed to Wagnerian aesthetics is an idea taken up in my essay 'Symphonic Opera, A Wagnerian Myth', in *Analysing Opera: Verdi and Wagner*, ed. Carolyn Abbate and Roger Parker (Berkeley: University of California Press, forthcoming).

20 Bernd Urban, in 'Hofmannsthal, Freud und die Psychoanalyse', *Literatur und Psychologie*, ed. Bernd Urban and Wolfram Mauser (Frankfurt am Main: Fischer, 1978), p. 36, has argued that Elektra's remark 'du liegst in deinem Selbst so eingekerkert' ('you are imprisoned within yourself') reflects her identification with Klytämnestra, as it is equally a description of the possessed daughter, who cannot be drawn by speech from the outside world.

21 Sigmund Freud and Josef Breuer, *Studien über Hysterie* (Frankfurt am Main, 1970), p. 47.

22 Strauss made one alteration in the structure of Hofmannsthal's version, in which the Young Servant sent to bring the news to Aegisthus interrupts Chrysothemis before her final lines 'Gestorben in der Fremde! tot! begraben dort in dem fremden Land' (etc.), which come as a resumption after the Servant's exit. Hofmannsthal had advised Strauss to eliminate the business of the Servant entirely (letter of 18 July 1906; *The Correspondence between Richard Strauss and Hugo von Hofmannsthal*, trans. Hanns Hammelmann and Ewald Osers (Cambridge: CUP, 1961), p. 8). Strauss instead shifted the interruption forward, to provide a black-comic buffer between Chrysothemis' narrative and Elektra's proposal that they themselves should be the avengers.

23 Arnold Schoenberg, *Theory of Harmony*, trans. Roy E. Carter (London: Faber, 1978), pp. 383–4.

24 The similarity of this flourish to the opera's opening bars is clear (and is reflected in Strauss's calculation of rehearsal numbers, which begin a second series with 1a at this point).

25 Cone, *The Composer's Voice*, p. 54.

26 See the chapter on *Tristan* in *Opera as Drama* (New York: Vintage, 1956), especially pp. 213–14.

8 The orchestration of *Elektra*: a critical interpretation

1 'Ten Golden Rules for the Album of a Young Conductor' (1925), in *Recollections and Reflections*, ed. Willi Schuh, trans. L. J. Lawrence (London: Boosey and Hawkes, 1953), p. 38.

2 Page references are to the miniature orchestral score and are used only when the rehearsal numbers common to both this and the piano score cannot suffice to make the location clear. Many of the points will of course be meaningless without an orchestral score.

3 Quotations from the libretto are given in the translation that accompanies the Solti recording (Decca SET 354–5).

4 Excepting, in the first, the more acrid bars when Elektra's pitying contempt turns Chrysothemis' music unwontedly baleful, and, in the second, Elektra's brief Salome-like blandishment of her sister's womanly charms.

5 Cf. also the bassoons' 'scale-practice' passages from four before Fig. 115 to Fig. 122.

6 Cf. Tethys Carpenter's (very different) account of this passage, pp. 82ff. [Ed.]

7 Many further points of detail exemplify the same acuity of ear. How well Strauss understands that difficult instrument the bass clarinet (compare Schoenberg, who always gets it so wrong). Not least at the very opening; the big D minor chord dies away leaving only bass clarinet and timp on the low tonic, together with a bass drum, so that when the timp disappears too the bass clarinet and bass drum fuse into a kind of bass timp in D over which the maid's first muttered words link daughter's name with father's theme. And how he understands the bass tuba in its tiny solo five bars after Fig. 39, when she thinks of her parents' royal bed, now so outraged.

8 Walter Piston, *Orchestration* (London: Gollancz, 1955).

9 'I cannot bear Strauss's six–four chords: *Ariadne* makes me want to scream.' Igor Stravinsky and Robert Craft, *Conversations with Igor Stravinsky* (London: Faber, 1959), p. 75.
10 Cf. Arnold Whittall above, pp. 69–70. [Ed.]
11 Most of the standard opera-house cuts are made in these two areas.
12 Cf. Romain Rolland:

> . . . I am in the process of reading the score of *Elektra*, by Richard Strauss, which has just been performed in Dresden. The materials are, as usual, rather (or very) vulgar; but one is swept along by the torrent. The libretto is much more beautiful than that of *Salomé*. That legend of the Atridae is in any case unfailingly moving; it exudes horror and a tragic pity which grip one irresistibly from the beginning to the end. Strauss himself has been caught by it (in spite of his nonchalance and Bavarian bantering which I, who know him well, come across endlessly in his ambling phrases and his eternal waltz rhythms, which he trails about everywhere with him, even at Agamemnon's: it's a very odd thing to see these German waltz rhythms transformed in his hands, and gradually translating with frenzied passion the transports of Elektra or of Clytemnestra).

> Letter to Paul Dupin, 13 February 1909, in *Richard Strauss and Romain Rolland: Correspondence, Diary and Essays*, ed. and annotated with a Preface by Rollo Myers (London: Calder and Boyars, 1968), p. 159.

13 See the present writer's chapter in *Richard Strauss: 'Salome'*, ed. Derrick Puffett (Cambridge: CUP, 1989).
14 'I still consider *Jeux* as an *orchestral* masterpiece, though I think some of the music is "*trop Lalique*".' *Conversations with Igor Stravinsky*, p. 50n.

Bibliography

Abert, Anna Amalie, *Richard Strauss: Die Opern* (Hanover: Friedrich, 1972)

Adorno, Theodor W., 'Richard Strauss', *Perspectives of New Music*, Vol. 4, No. 1 (Fall–Winter 1965), pp. 14–32; No. 2 (Spring–Summer 1966), pp. 113–29

Anon, 'Richard Strauss' *Elektra*' (report of interview), *Allgemeine Musikzeitung* [Berlin], 25 September 1908, p. 669

Asow, Erich H. Mueller von, *Richard Strauss: Thematisches Verzeichnis*, 3 vols. (Vienna and Wiesbaden: Doblinger, 1959–74), Vol. 1 (Opp. 1–59), pp. 399–441 (on *Elektra*)

Baumann, Gerhart, 'Hugo von Hofmannsthal: *Elektra*', *Germanisch-Romanische Monatsschrift*, Vol. 9 (1959)

Beecham, Sir Thomas, *A Mingled Chime* (London: Hutchinson, 1944), pp. 89–92 (on *Elektra*)

Bekker, Paul, '*Elektra*: Studie', *Neue Musik-Zeitung*, Vol. 30 (1909), pp. 293, 330, 387

Brosche, Günter, *Richard Strauss: Bibliographie* (Vienna: Brüder Hollinek, 1973)

Brosche, Günter, and Dachs, Karl, *Richard Strauss: Autographen in München und Wien: Verzeichnis* (Tutzing: Schneider, 1979)

Cohn, Hilde D., 'Hofmannsthals Libretti', *German Quarterly*, Vol. 35 (1962)

Conrad, Peter, *Romantic Opera and Literary Form* (Berkeley: University of California Press, 1977)

Craft, Robert, *Current Convictions: Views and Reviews* (London: Secker and Warburg, 1978), especially the essays 'A "Beautiful Coloured, Musical Thing"' (on *Salome*), '*Der Rosenkavalier*: "Something Mozartian"?', '*Elektra* and Richard Strauss'

Dahlhaus, Carl, *Die Musik des 19. Jahrhunderts* (Wiesbaden: Akademische Verlagsgesellschaft Athenaion, 1980), pp. 291–3 (on *Elektra*)

Daviau, Donald G., and Buelow, George J., *The 'Ariadne auf Naxos' of Hugo von Hofmannsthal and Richard Strauss* (Chapel Hill: University of North Carolina Press, 1975)

Del Mar, Norman, *Richard Strauss: A Critical Commentary on His Life and Works*, 3 vols. (London: Barrie and Jenkins, 1978)

Dinerstein, Norman M., 'Polychordality in *Salome* and *Elektra*: A Study of the Application of Re-Interpretation Technique' (Unpublished Ph.D. Diss., Princeton University, 1974)

Einstein, Alfred, 'Strauss und Hofmannsthal', in *Von Schütz bis Hindemith* (Zurich, 1957)

Enix, Margery A., 'The Dissolution of the Functional Harmonic Tonal System: 1850–1910' (Unpublished Ph.D. Diss., University of Indiana, 1977), pp. 362–415 (on *Elektra*)

'A Reassessment of *Elektra*', *Indiana Theory Review*, Vol. 2 (1979)

Erwin, Charlotte E., 'Richard Strauss's Presketch Planning for *Ariadne auf Naxos*', *Musical Quarterly*, Vol. 67, No. 3 (July 1981)

Ewans, Michael, 'Elektra: Sophokles, Von Hofmannsthal, Strauss', *Ramus*, Vol. 13, No. 2 (1984)

Finck, Henry T., *Richard Strauss: The Man and the Works* (Boston: Little, Brown and Co., 1917)

Fischer-Planer, Ernst, *Einführung in die Musik von Richard Strauss und Elektra* (Leipzig: Reform, 1909)

Forsyth, Karen, *'Ariadne auf Naxos' by Hugo von Hofmannsthal and Richard Strauss: Its Genesis and Meaning* (London: OUP, 1982)

Gerlach, Reinhard, *Don Juan und Rosenkavalier: Studien zu Idee und Gestalt einer tonalen Evolution im Werk Richard Strauss* (Berne: Haupt, 1966)

Gilliam, Bryan, 'Strauss's Preliminary Opera Sketches: Thematic Fragments and Symphonic Continuity', *Nineteenth-Century Music*, Vol. 9, No. 3 (Spring 1986)

Gollob, H., *Richard Wagner und Richard Strauss in der musikalischen Malerei* (Vienna: Gerold, 1957)

Gould, Glenn, 'An Argument for Richard Strauss', in *The Glenn Gould Reader*, ed. Tim Page (London: Faber, 1987)

Grainger, Percy, 'Richard Strauss: Seer and Idealist', in Finck, Henry T., *Richard Strauss: The Man and the Works* (Boston: Little, Brown and Co., 1917)

Grasberger, Franz, *Richard Strauss und die Wiener Oper* (Tutzing: Schneider, 1969)

Grasberger, Franz, ed., *Der Strom der Töne trug mich fort: Die Welt um Richard Strauss in Briefen* (Tutzing: Schneider, 1967)

Hartmann, Rudolf, *Richard Strauss: The Staging of His Operas and Ballets*, trans. Graham Davies (Oxford: Phaidon Press, 1982)

Hofmannsthal, Hugo von, *Elektra: Tragödie in einem Aufzug* (first edition) (Berlin: Fischer, 1904)

Briefe 1900–1909 (Vienna: Bermann-Fischer Verlag, 1937)

Elektra: Tragödie in einem Aufzug frei nach Sophokles, in *Gesammelte Werke: Dramen II*, ed. Bernd Schoeller (Frankfurt am Main: Fischer, 1979)

Holländer, Hans, 'Hugo von Hofmannsthal als Opernlibrettist', *Neue Zeitschrift für Musik*, Vol. 96 (1929)

Holloway, Robin, 'Strauss's Last Opera', *Music and Musicians*, Vol. 21, No. 12 (August 1973)

Hutcheson, E., *Elektra by Richard Strauss: A Guide to the Opera with Musical Examples from the Score* (New York, 1910)

Jaacks, Gisela, and Jahnke, Andres W., eds., *Richard Strauss (1864–1949): 'Musik des Lichts in dunkler Zeit': Vom Bürgerschreck zum Rosenkavalier* (Mainz: Schott, 1979)

Jefferson, Alan, *The Operas of Richard Strauss in Britain 1910–1963* (London: Putnam, 1963), pp. 17–35 (on *Elektra*)

Jens, Walther, *Hofmannsthal und die Griechen* (Tübingen, 1955)

Kaplan, Richard A., 'The Musical Language of *Elektra*: A Study in Chromatic Harmony' (Unpublished Ph.D. Diss., University of Michigan, 1985)

Kennedy, Michael, *Richard Strauss* (London: Dent, 1976)

'Richard Strauss' (with worklist by Robert Bailey), in *The New Grove Dictionary of Music and Musicians*, ed. Stanley Sadie, 20 vols. (London: Macmillan, 1980)

Klein, Walter, 'Die Harmonisation in *Elektra* von Richard Strauss: Ein Beitrag zur modernen Harmonisationslehre', *Der Merker*, Vol. 2, Nos. 12–14 (1911), pp. 512–14, 540–3, 590–2

Knaus, Jakob, *Hofmannsthals Weg zur Oper 'Die Frau ohne Schatten': Rücksichte und Einflüsse auf die Musik* (Berlin: de Gruyter, 1971)

Kralik, Heinrich, *Richard Strauss: Weltbürger der Musik* (Vienna: Wollzeilen, 1963)

Krause, Ernst, *Richard Strauss: The Man and His Work* (London: Collet, 1964)

Krüger, Karl-Joachim, *Hugo von Hofmannsthal und Richard Strauss* (Berlin, 1935)

Lewis, Hannah B., '*Salome* and *Elektra*: Sisters or Strangers', *Orbis Literarum*, Vol. 31, No. 1 (1976)

Mahler, Alma, *Gustav Mahler: Memories and Letters*, trans. Basil Creighton, ed. Donald Mitchell, 3rd edn (London: Faber, 1973)

Gustav Mahler–Richard Strauss: Correspondence 1888–1911, ed. with notes and an essay by Herta Blaukopf, trans. Edmund Jephcott (London: Faber, 1984)

Mann, William, 'A Note on *Elektra*', *Musical Times*, Vol. 95, No. 1336 (1954)

Richard Strauss: A Critical Study of the Operas (London: Cassell, 1964)

Marek, George R., *Richard Strauss: The Life of a Non-Hero* (London, 1967)

Mayer, Hans, 'Hugo von Hofmannsthal und Richard Strauss', in *Ansichten zur Literatur der Zeit* (Hamburg, 1962)

McDonald, Lawrence F., 'Compositional Procedures in Richard Strauss' *Elektra*' (Unpublished Ph.D. Diss., University of Michigan, 1976)

McMullen, Sally, 'From the Armchair to the Stage: Hofmannsthal's *Elektra* in Its Theatrical Context', *Modern Language Review*, Vol. 80, No. 3 (July 1985)

Newman, Ernest, *Richard Strauss* (London: John Lane, 1908; repr. 1970)

Opera Nights (London: Putnam, 1943), pp. 146–61 (on *Elektra*)

Testament of Music (London: Putnam, 1963)

Noé, Günther von, 'Das Leitmotiv in Richard Straussens *Elektra*', *Das neue Forum*, Vol. 9 (1959–60)

Overhoff, Kurt, *Die Elektra-Partitur von Richard Strauss: Ein Lehrbuch für die Technik der dramatischen Komposition* (Salzburg: Pustet, 1978)

Panofsky, Walter, *Richard Strauss: Partitur eines Lebens* (Darmstadt: Deutsche Buch-Gemeinschaft, 1965)

Pantle, Sherrill Hahn, *'Die Frau ohne Schatten' by Hugo von Hofmannsthal and Richard Strauss: An Analysis of Text, Music and Their Relationship* (Berne: Lang, 1978)

Politzer, Heinz, 'Hofmannsthal und die Oper', *Forum*, Vol. 2 (1955)

'Hugo von Hofmannsthals "Elektra": Geburt der Tragödie aus dem Geiste der Psychopathologie', *Deutsche Vierteljahresschrift für Literaturwissenschaft und Geistesgeschichte*, Vol. 47 (1973)

Polower, Genie Edith, 'Hofmannsthal as Librettist' (Unpublished M. A. Diss., Rutgers University, 1976)

Puffett, Derrick, 'An Introduction to *Der Rosenkavalier*', in *Der Rosenkavalier*, ed. Nicholas John (London: John Calder, 1981)

Puffett, Derrick, ed., *Richard Strauss: 'Salome'* (Cambridge: CUP, 1989)

Röse, Otto, and Prüwer, Julius, *Elektra: Ein Musikführer durch das Werk* (Berlin: Fürstner, 1909)

Roth, Ernst, ed., *Richard Strauss Stage Works: Documents of the First Performances* (London: Boosey and Hawkes, 1954)

Schmidgall, Gary, *Literature as Opera* (New York: OUP, 1977)

Schnitzler, Günter, 'Kongenialität und Divergenz: Zum Eingang der Oper *Elektra* von Hugo von Hofmannsthal und Richard Strauss', in *Dichtung und Musik*, ed. Günter Schnitzler (Stuttgart: Klett-Cotta, 1979)

Schuch, Friedrich von, *Richard Strauss, Ernst von Schuch und Dresdens Oper*, 2nd edn (Leipzig: Verlag der Kunst, 1953)

Schuh, Willi, *Über Opern von Richard Strauss* (Zurich: Atlantis, 1947)

The Stage Works of Richard Strauss (London: Boosey and Hawkes, 1954)

Hugo von Hofmannsthal und Richard Strauss: Legende und Wirklichkeit (Munich: Hanser, 1964); repr. in *Umgang mit Musik* (Zurich: Atlantis, 1970)

Straussiana aus vier Jahrzehnten (Tutzing: Schneider, 1981)

Richard Strauss: A Chronicle of the Early Years (1864-1898), trans. Mary Whittall (Cambridge: CUP, 1982)

Schuh, Willi, and Roth, Ernst, *Richard Strauss: Complete Catalogue* (London: Boosey and Hawkes, 1964)

Segar, Kenneth, 'Hofmannsthal's *Elektra*: From Drama to Libretto', in *'Salome' and 'Elektra'*, ed. Nicholas John (London: John Calder, 1988)

Smith, Patrick J., *The Tenth Muse: A Historical Study of the Opera Libretto* (London: Gollancz, 1971)

Specht, Richard, *Richard Strauss und sein Werk*, 2 vols. (Leipzig, Vienna and Zurich: E. P. Tal & Co., 1921), especially Vol. 2, pp. 165-214 (on *Elektra*)

Steingruber, Elisabeth, *Hugo von Hofmannsthals Sophokleische Dramen* (Winterthur, 1956)

Steinitzer, Max, *Richard Strauss* (Berlin: Schuster and Loeffler, 1911)

Strauss, Richard, *Recollections and Reflections*, ed. Willi Schuh, trans. L. J. Lawrence (London: Boosey and Hawkes, 1953)

Richard Strauss and Romain Rolland: Correspondence, Diary and Essays, ed. and annotated with a Preface by Rollo Myers (London: Calder and Boyars, 1968)

Richard Strauss: Briefwechsel mit Willi Schuh, ed. Willi Schuh (Zurich: Atlantis, 1969)

Richard Strauss und Hugo von Hofmannsthal: Briefwechsel: Gesamtausgabe, ed. Willi Schuh, 5th edn (Zurich: Atlantis, 1978) (includes letters not in the English edition)

The Correspondence between Richard Strauss and Hugo von Hofmannsthal, trans. Hanns Hammelmann and Ewald Osers (Cambridge: CUP, 1980)

Tenschert, Roland, *Dreimal sieben Variationen über das Thema Richard Strauss* (Vienna: Frick, 1944)

Trenner, Franz, *Richard Strauss: Dokumente seines Lebens und Schaffens* (Munich: C. H. Beck, 1954)

Die Skizzenbücher von Richard Strauss aus dem Richard-Strauss-Archiv in Garmisch (Tutzing: Schneider, 1977), pp. 28–32, 163–5 (on *Elektra*)

Wellesz, Egon, *Essays on Opera*, trans. Patricia Kean (London: Dennis Dobson, 1950), pp. 113–15 (on *Elektra*)

Wilhelm, Kurt, *Richard Strauss persönlich: Eine Bildbiographie* (Munich: Kindler, 1984)

Winterhager, Wolfgang, *Zur Struktur des Operndialogs: Komparative Analysen des musikdramatischen Werks von Richard Strauss* (Frankfurt: Lang, 1984)

Wintle, Christopher, 'Elektra and the "Elektra Complex"', in *'Salome' and 'Elektra'*, ed. Nicholas John (London: John Calder, 1988)

Discography

MALCOLM WALKER

E	Elektra	(m)	mono recording
C	Chrysothemis	(4)	cassette version
K	Klytämnestra	CD	Compact Disc version
A	Aegisthus	(e)	electronically reprocessed stereo
O	Orestes	*	78 rpm record
		CDV	Compact Disc Video

All recordings in stereo unless otherwise stated. The dates quoted relate to the year of recording.

'Complete' recordings

Note: Only the Solti recording is absolutely complete. All other performances contain cuts.

1937   (concert performance: Carnegie Hall, New York) Pauly *E*; Boerner *C*; Szantho *K*; Jagel *A*; Huehn *O*; New York PSO / Rodzinski
           Golden Age of Opera (m) EJS145
           Unique Opera Recording (m) UORC322
    (NB: Although this recording is abridged, the disc contains all of Elektra's role)

1943   Schlüter *E*; Kupper *C*; Von Ilosvay *K*; Markworth *A*; Neidlinger *O*; Hamburg State Opera Chorus & Orch / Jochum
           Acanta (m) 40.23073

1947   (broadcast performance: BBC Studios, Maida Vale, London) Schlüter *E*; Welitsch *C*; Höngen *K*; Widdop *A*; Schoeffler *O*; BBC Theatre Chorus / RPO / Beecham
           Cetra (m) ARK9
           Melodram (m) MEL041

1950   (public performance: Maggio Musicale Fiorentino) A. Konetzni *E*; Ilitsch *C*; Mödl *K*; Klarwein *A*; Braun *O*; Maggio Musicale Fiorentino Chorus & Orch / Mitropoulos
           Cetra (m) OLPC1209
           Turnabout (e) THS65040

1952   (public performance: Metropolitan Opera House, New York) Varnay *E*; Wegner *C*; Höngen *K*; Svanholm *A*; Schoeffler *O*; Metropolitan Opera Chorus & Orch / Reiner
           Rococo (m) RR1101

1953   (broadcast performance: WDR Cologne) Varnay *E*; Rysanek *C*;
        R. Fischer *K*; Melchert *A*; Hotter *O*; Cologne Radio Chorus &
        SO / R. Kraus

        Melodram (m) MEL112

1957   (public performance: Salzburg Festival) Borkh *E*; Della Casa *C*;
        Madeira *K*; Lorenz *A*; Böhme *O*; Vienna State Opera Chorus /
        VPO / Mitropoulos

        Cetra (m) LO83
        CD: Melodram 37008

1960   Borkh *E*; Schech *C*; Madeira *K*; Uhl *A*; Fischer-Dieskau *O*;
        Dresden State Opera Chorus / Staatskapelle Dresden / Böhm

        DG 2721 187

1964   (public performance: Salzburg Festival) Varnay *E*; Hillebrecht *C*;
        Mödl *K*; King *A*; Waechter *O*; Vienna State Opera Chorus / VPO /
        Karajan

        Estro Armonico (m) EA044

1965   (public performance: Staatsoper, Vienna) Nilsson *E*; Rysanek *C*;
        Resnik *K*; Windgassen *A*; Waechter *O*; Vienna State Opera Chorus
        & Orch / Böhm

        Historical Recording Enterprises (m)
        HRE314

1966/7 Nilsson *E*; Collier *C*; Resnik *K*; Stolze *A*; Krause *O*; Vienna State
        Opera Chorus / VPO / Solti

        Decca SET353/4 (4) K124K22
        CD: 414 345–2DH2
        London OSA1269
        CD: 414 345–2LH2

?1970/1 (public performances: Staatsoper, Hamburg) Kuchta *E*; Bjöner *C*;
        Resnik *K*; Melchert *A*; Sotin *O*; Hamburg State Opera Chorus /
        Hamburg Philharmonic State Orch / Ludwig

        'private label' GK 1/4 (4 sides)

1981   (Unitel film) Rysanek *E*; Ligendza *C*; Varnay *K*; Beirer *A*; Fischer-
        Dieskau *O*; Vienna State Opera Chorus / VPO / Böhm

        CDV: Decca 071 400–1DH2

1984   (concert performance: French Radio) Vinzing *E*; Rysanek *C*; For-
        rester *K*; Hiestermann *A*; Norup *O*; French Radio Chorus / French
        National Orch / Perick

        Rodolphe RP12420
        CD: RPC32420

1988   (concert performances) Behrens *E*; Secunde *C*; Ludwig *K*; Ulfung
        A; Hynninen *O*; Tanglewood Festival Chorus / Boston SO /
        Ozawa

        CD: Philips 422 574–2PH2

Excerpts

Final Scene

1947   Schlüter *E*; Welitsch *C*; Höngen *K*; Widdop *A*; Schoeffler *O*; BBC
        Theatre Chorus / RPO / Beecham
                            RCA (UK) (m) RL42821
                            (US) LCT1135
        (NB: This begins at the recognition scene and continues to the end
        of the opera. There are two small cuts.)

'Allein! Weh, ganz allein' (Elektra's Monologue)

1950s   Varnay (Orch / ?Weigert)
                            Estro Armonico (m) EA35
1951   Varnay: Orch niederösterreichischer Tonkünstler / Weigert
                            Acanta (m) 22645
1952   Goltz; Bavarian State Opera Orch / Solti
                            DG (m) LPM18090
                            US Decca (m) DL9723
1956   Borkh; Chicago SO / Reiner
                            RCA (US) CD: 5603-2RC
1968   Shuard; Royal Opera House Orch, Covent Garden / Solti
                            Decca SET392/3
                            London OSA1276

'Was willst du, fremder Mensch?' (Recognition Scene)

1953   Goltz; Franz; Bavarian State Opera Orch / Solti
                            DG (m) LPEM19038
                            US Decca (m) DL9723
1956   Borkh; Schoeffler; Chicago SO / Reiner
                            RCA (US) CD: 5603-2RC
1964   Ludwig; Berry; Orch der Deutschen Oper, Berlin / Hollreiser
                            World Record Club SCM84
                            RCA (US) VICS1269

'Elektra! Schwester!' (Finale)

1956   Borkh; Yeend; Chicago Lyric Theater Chorus / Chicago SO /
        Reiner
                            RCA (US) CD: 5603-2RC

Index

18" x 38"
6 PANES

35 5/8"

17"

Frued — Hystaria.